<u>Revved Up Real Estate:</u>

<u>The Mindsets and Systems that Doubled My Dealflow</u>

Colley Bailey

ISBN: 9798374918359

Printed and manufactured in the United States of America

First Edition

Author: Colley Bailey

Editor: Amanda Lee-Bailey

Table of Contents

Acknowledgements

I first want to thank you, the reader, for picking up this book and giving me a chance to tell my story. I hope it changes your life on a grand scale. I hope this information has even more impact on your life than it had on mine.

Next, I must thank my incredible wife, Amanda. Babe, I absolutely adore you. You're my Ride or Die, my Muse, my Empress. There have been so many times you believed in me when I wasn't even sure I believed in myself. So much of who I am, who I have become, is because of you.

I need to thank my parents for raising me with great values, a hard work ethic, and good self-esteem. You've loved and supported me through all my crazy schemes and dreams. And I couldn't be more grateful to you all.

Thank you to Joshua Harley, who's built an unbelievable opportunity in Fathom Realty. Thanks to James Dray for believing in me enough to hire me (twice.) Thanks to John Rausch for giving me the opportunity of a lifetime, and inspiring me to rise to the occasion. Thanks to Lance Drinkard for the tough love coaching. You've all made me a better professional.

Over the years, I've bought countless courses, consumed hundreds of hours of content, and learned from the best coaches & mentors across the sales, marketing, real estate, and business niches. I've learned significant lessons from the following professionals:

Krista Mashore, Grant Wise, Sherri Johnson & Jill Katzenberg, Roland Frasier, Matt McCutcheon, Ryan Fletcher, Greg Luther, Jeff Shore, Will Penney, Dan Lok, Chris Voss, Joshua Smith, Jon Cheplak, Grant Cardone, Alex Hormozi, Gary Vaynerchuk, Patrick Bet-David, Ricky Carruth, Tristan Ahumada, Kevin Ward, Knolly Williams, Michael Reese, Hoss Pratt, Greg Hague, David Prulhiere, Kathleen Everitt, Larry Kelley, Matt Mulson, Stephanie Back, Lance Martin, Landon Ward, Ramon Pineda, Ngoma Hantuba, Randy Ross, Brian Kirk, Luther Keeling, Eric Hutchinson, Mark Flake, Chris Bogner, Sean Kaiser, Tara Limbird, and Eric Ravenscroft.

I'm inspired by and extremely grateful to you all! Thank you.

Introduction:
The Route I Took

I cracked the code. I figured it out. I finally made it happen.

Over the course of two years, I had successfully doubled my transaction volume every six months.

The goal had gone from generating Half a Million Dollars in Volume from January to July, then One Million Dollars from July to January, then $2M by the next July, then $4M by January. And at every 6 month mark, I had hit each one of those goals.

I had been a top producer before (previously being a part of a high-volume new construction sales team), but this was different. This was me all on my own. This was a brand new system in action, a system I had built for myself. I had carved out my own clientele from the marketplace, and created a self-scaling business for the first time in my life.

In that second year, I was able to generate almost $200,000 in gross commissions, a goal I'd wanted to hit for almost 7 years at that time. It felt amazing to cross that off my list.

That being said, I'm no guru. I'm not the #1 Real Estate Agent in the U.S., or even my own state. Many top agents in higher priced markets around the country could look at those results and laugh at how small the numbers are.

But I was immensely proud. Because the system worked. And it was mine.

To be clear, I haven't "made it" yet. I'm just a hard working guy from humble beginnings who's constantly striving toward ever more ambitious aims. My goals are now much larger, both in income, and in impact. I haven't arrived at any sort of final destination. I'm still on my way. (And maybe you can join me on this journey.)

But, if you're looking to grow your real estate business with a simple system that can deliver consistent results, then look no further. This book is for you.

Growing Up

You see, I grew up in a mobile home on a small 19 acre horse farm, 10 miles outside the nearest town of 2,000 people. That little town was called Flippin, Arkansas. It's biggest claim to fame was the Ranger Boat factory, started by a gentleman named Forrest Wood.

He pretty much singlehandedly invented the modern Bass fishing boat and spawned an entirely new industry, sponsoring professional fishermen and fishing tournaments around the country. I met him a few times as a kid, and even got an autograph. Just knowing that he'd done something so big gave me hope that I could do something big with my life too.

I came from generations of hardworking, blue-collar Ozark Mountain folks. My step-father is a master-level machinist. My grandfather ran his own radiator repair shop. My other grandfather had been a stone mason. My dad had been a pipeliner, and my uncle ran his own cabinet shop. Even my mother spent a few years as a truck driver.

I was always surrounded by people with high work ethic and systems thinking. Several generations of my family and many of my cousins are auto mechanics, and working with "systems" seem to come so naturally to them: the ability to see how one piece of an engine interacts with the others, how everything works together to make it run, and to troubleshoot problems and solutions within the system. I definitely got some of those hard working, system seeing genes as well.

As I got into my teenage years, I found myself wanting to apply that work ethic to school and use my head, not just my hands. This lead me to study hard and graduate at the top of my class. I was voted "most likely to succeed," eventually landing a full ride to college on academic scholarships.

When I think of back home, I often think of watching the IMCA Modified race cars at the local oval dirt track, the North Central Arkansas Speedway. I can still smell the grease and hear the metal clanking in the garage as my uncle and his sons built their cars, gearing up for the weekend thrillrides. And I remember the deafening roar of the engines on those summer nights as the cars blasted down the track and threw their tires sideways into the big looping corners. As a kid, I loved sitting in those stands, with cotton balls for ear plugs, having my whole body shaken to the bone by the thundering engines.

I guess the love of the thrill, the chase of adrenaline, and the desire to "REV THINGS UP" never really left me. (Which might explain the race car metaphors throughout the book)

Rock Bottom

I'm writing this book to give you a little guidance and share what finally worked for me. And hopefully to save you from hitting rock bottom like I did...

It was 2017. I was two years into my real estate career and I was desperately trying not to become a statistic. You know the one I'm talking about: the fact that 87% of agents that fail out in the first three years of their careers.

I spent the first year of my career working part time, and doing open houses almost every weekend. It took eleven months to get my first commission check, which was only about $3,000.

Luckily, by year two, I had enough clients in the pipeline that I felt comfortable going full time. And for the first part of that year, I made pretty good money. But then the deal flow ran dry. That fall, I started knocking on doors around Fayetteville to try and meet homeowners that might sell. I ended up knocking on 3,000 doors in an attempt to scrounge up a deal.

But, I didn't really know what I was doing. I didn't have sales skills. I had no real offer. And I had no real advertising budget. It was looking dismal.

To make matters worse, we were relying on my parents to pay the bills. And it had been that way for months. Here I was, a 32 year old man, begging for money from my parents, and begging for business at people's front doors.

Mentally, I was drowning, and my wife Amanda could only stand by and watch me circle the drain. We had two young daughters (5 and 2) at the time and we were living in a cramped little duplex on a drug infested street in one of the only bad parts of an otherwise good town. There were three shootings in that neighborhood during the time we lived there. So, as you can imagine, we were desperate to get our young family out of that situation. We felt every day we stayed in that duplex was dangerous.

And finally, Amanda had enough. I came home from knocking on doors begging for business, and she said,

"That's it! You have to get a job. Just a normal, regular job with a steady paycheck."

The next part hit me like a ton of bricks:

"I can't do this anymore. Either get a job, or I'm leaving."

. . . . . . I couldn't talk. . . . . . I couldn't breathe.

My heart sank into my hips. It was at that point I finally got it. I had failed. I didn't know what I was doing, and I wasn't providing for my family like they deserved.

As I left the room, something came over me. Anger. But I wasn't mad at her. She was right to doubt me, as I had proven over and over again. I was mad at myself. Deep bubbling, boiling anger. This wasn't how I wanted our life to be. This wasn't how I wanted it to end.

I burst back into the room and forcefully declared,

"If you leave me right now, it will be the worst mistake of your life.

I WILL BE SUCCESSFUL!!!

I WILL make this work! I WILL figure it out! I WILL build the life we've always dreamed about. And I want you to be there with me to get it.

If you leave right now, you'll always kick yourself for giving up too soon. Because I WILL be successful. And I'd rather do it with you than without you."

The truth is, I was terrified she would leave. I was terrified of living life alone, without her. She was everything to me.

But I couldn't give up. Not again. Not ever again.

Hollywood

You see, Amanda and I had been through failure before.

We started dating right after she graduated from the University of Arkansas. I had graduated from University of Central Arkansas a year prior. We really got swept up in each other and our whirlwind romance led to us getting married just 5 months later. I knew she was the one.

The next year, we moved to Los Angeles so I could pursue my big dream of becoming a film actor. Amanda was my biggest fan, and she believed I could do it. She pushed me to go for it.

We hit the ground running. Within weeks, I was getting booked as a background actor on every major movie studio lot in Hollywood (CBS, Warner Brothers, Paramount, Universal, etc). It became my day job. I got to be on set for some of the biggest shows and movies of the time (2009-2010):

- GLEE
- Greek
- Rizzoli & Isles
- Grey's Anatomy
- Hot Tub Time Machine
- Just Go With It

Amanda also got a full time job as an assistant at a home health agency and carried the bulk of our bills. This freed me up to go to my auditions and attend acting classes.

I was lucky enough to be accepted into Ivana Chubbuck Studios in West Hollywood. Ivana was the acting coach to the stars, with several notable students including Brad Pitt, Charlize Theron, Orlando Bloom, Halle Berry, and the list goes on. I got to work on my craft with some incredible coaches and worked with some amazing fellow actors there.

With a lot of luck and quite a bit of hard work, I landed leading roles in two Independent Horror movies: **Donner Pass** and **Madison County**. (Yes, you can look me up on IMDB, Amazon, Netflix, etc)

Through my connections, I was able to get a unique insight into the back end of the movie business. As a side hustle, I had been doing website design for a Casting Director Workshop. With this connection, I met some of the biggest casting directors in the industry. For reference, movie producers hire *these* casting directors to hold auditions and to help decide on the best actors for all the roles in some of the biggest films and shows produced.

And what they shared with me was astounding. When they put out an audition announcement for a small role on the casting portals, they get a flood of responses, like 10,000 applicants for a small speaking part that might only film for one day. So, they just comb through the headshots to see who jumps out at them. They whittle it down to a few hundred, just from one photo of each actor (the headshot.) Then they have auditions for a hundred or so actors. Then callbacks for the top twenty or so. And then the producers and directors might see the top 5-10 actors. And then one is chosen and offered the role.

The odds started to mess with my head. One in Ten Thousand. For. Every. Role.

And then I started looking around LA, and I saw versions of myself everywhere. When I went to auditions, I was walking into a room full of 100 guys who looked just like me, except most were taller and in better shape. At the grocery store, guys who looked like future versions of me, who had been there for a few decades, and never "made it." Everywhere I looked, I saw people who had tried to hit it big in Hollywood, but who would probably never see the limelight.

I couldn't stand the idea of depending on some casting director to "pull my lucky number." I didn't want my life to be a lottery. Amanda and I wanted a family. We wanted a home, not just a cramped studio apartment on Hollywood and Normandie. We wanted to travel and do exciting things. The longer I chased auditions, feeling that searing sting of rejection each time, the more I could feel the "Hollywood Dream" smothering the "American Dream" we also wanted so badly.

Oh, and the Los Angeles traffic sucked. Really bad.

By 2011, I had an idea for a movie script I wanted to produce, and I convinced myself it could be made back home in Arkansas. So, we left.

After lots of remote video auditions, a few flights back to LA for the big auditions (notably, 50 Shades of Gray), and one more movie role in an Arkansas Indy called *Valley Inn*, I'd had enough. Also, I wasn't finding investors to help fund the film I left LA to produce.

I was ready to let it go. I needed to take back my power and sense of self-worth from the ruthless audition process. I gave up the Hollywood dream.

Failure After Failure

In the years following LA, I drifted from job to job, aimlessly searching for something to pursue that felt worthwhile. I needed to find myself again. But mostly, I was just trying to scratch out a living and provide for my young family. Our first daughter, Layla, was born within the first year upon coming back to Arkansas. As any first time father can attest to, that immense feeling of responsibility hits hard when you hold your baby for the first time. You better get your act together because now life is REAL!

I tried being a carpenter, a restaurant manager, an electrician, I even tried to put my Hollywood skills to use by starting a small photo & video production company.

But ultimately, nothing was really a good fit. And nothing was providing a good living. We were BROKE. All the time.

Eventually, I started doing photography for some local real estate agents, and one of them convinced me to get my license. My step-dad said he'd cover the cost of classes, and I was on my way.

Two years later, we found ourselves at that Rock Bottom moment. Amanda had seen SEVEN YEARS of failures before finally asking me to throw in the towel, to give in and get a standard corporate job. She knew I was smart and capable enough to make it. So why hadn't I amounted to something more than begging my dad for money every month?

I was supposed to be her Movie Star, but by that point I was just a Mess.

My Breakthrough

We did ultimately compromise. I said I'd get a W2 job, as long as it was in the real estate space. I was putting a flag in the ground. I was not leaving this industry, no matter what. No more giving up!

Not long after that, I interviewed and got offered a position selling new construction homes for Arkansas and Oklahoma's largest home builder. It was just the chance we needed. I poured everything I had into being a great new home salesperson. I was off to the races!

Within a few years on that high-producing team, I had helped them sell through over 4 neighborhoods worth of homes. I was ranked as a Top 100 Residential Agent in the *Northwest Arkansas Business Journal*, and one of Arkansas' Best Realtors® in the state's *About You Magazine.* Most importantly, I was finally able to have a home built for my family in one of the neighborhoods I was selling at the time. No more "danger duplex"

I had finally learned:

- How to Generate Leads
- How to Follow Up most Effectively
- How to Convert Leads into Clients and Advise them Accordingly
- How to Give Great Customer Service throughout the Transaction
- How to Handle Large Volumes of Contracts
- How to Get Great Reviews

15

Like my cousins back home tuning their engines, these were the components of my business I'd used to craft a successful career. Those were the 6 Cylinders of My Income Engine, and they'll soon be yours if you follow me through the rest of this book.

I'll be forever grateful to that employer. They gave me a chance that changed my life forever. That team will always hold a special place in my heart.

Eventually, the time came for me to strike out on my own. As a team, we had sold through a record number of homes that year, but we were left with a sizable dent in the number of lots we'd be able to build houses on within the year to come. Taking a glance at the lot counts, I knew our business would decline next year, and some of us wouldn't have anything to sell. Decidedly, when I sold through the last few lots in the neighborhood I'd been assigned, I opted to start my new venture instead of putting more strain on my teammates.

It was almost as if I'd been quietly building a Hot-Rod in my garage, one part at a time, for the last few years. A lead generation engine here, a sales transmission there, etc. And now the time had come to fire that baby up and go racing.

It worked. In the first 6 months, I only sold $588,000 in volume. (Oh and a global pandemic was announced during that time.) The next 6 months, I sold $1.54 Million in volume. In another half year, I'd logged $2.27M. And to round out the following 6 months, I ended up with $3.998M. I doubled my sales volume goal every 6 months, and I hit those goals for 2 years straight!

And it was all from my own efforts, my own systems this time. Indeed I had figured it out, and my career was firing on all cylinders.

With this book, I hope to guide you in building a Real Estate Race Car of your own so you can join me on the track.

Rev that Engine! Let's Go For a Ride!

Part 1:
Rules of the Road

Overview

In order to drive your Real Estate Race Car, you need to understand the engine that powers your business.

Think of the engine as a system of interconnected parts that delivers a desired output. In our case, Profit is the output.

When most agents try to conceptualize building a successful business, it looks complex, messy, and overwhelming. It seems impossible. Maybe something like this:

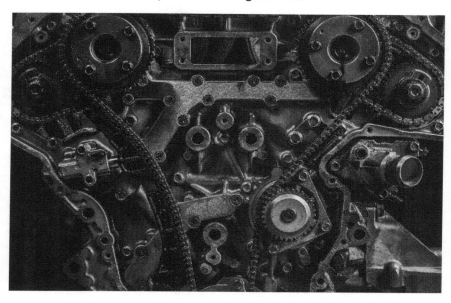

My job throughout this book is to simplify the chaos, to break this business down into its component parts so you understand what's working and what isn't. I can guarantee that if your engine isn't firing on all cylinders, your business won't run very long. It might not start up in the first place.

So with that in mind, let me introduce you to the 6 Cylinder Powerplant driving your business forward.

These are the main pistons involved in powering the engine of your Real Estate business:

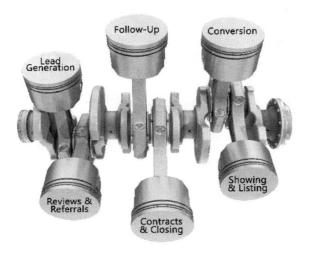

Later, we'll add more components to your business, like this:

Pretty soon, you'll be lapping your competition with a Supercharged V6 Race Winning Rocket like this:

For ease of use throughout this book, we'll be representing our business engine with this diagram, which provides the simple framework of a 6 cylinder, clockwise-rotating, self-sustaining cycle:

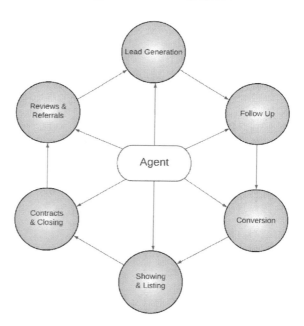

This is what we'll spend the rest of the book exploring in detail. (And yes, that's you in the middle there.) I'll teach you to keep this engine firing on all cylinders!

Mindsets

To successfully drive your Real Estate Career and keep all 6 cylinders operating optimally, we must start with you. Specifically, we need to examine your thoughts, beliefs, and perspectives around your own success. That's what this chapter is all about.

Throw out your old rulebook. This book is a new set of rules for real estate today. We're not in a 1950's clunker, we're in a High Performance Speedster and your mindset has to reflect that. I'm going to help you see your professional self in a different light. That all starts with your mind.

Having the right mindset is critical if you want to make an impact, grow your income, and own your destiny. It's been a constantly evolving journey for me, working on my confidence and trying to think my way through solving life's problems.

"Do what you can, with what you've got, where you are." – **Theodore Roosevelt**

Like Roosevelt indicated above, the only place to start is where you are, and start now, with whatever you've got. For me, I didn't have a lot, but the following mindsets helped me get to where I am now.

You need to see your professional self in a new light, and the following perspective shifts will lead you to higher and higher levels of performance. Quite often, when you're feeling stuck in your career, all you need is a new mindset to push into a new level of growth. Always be evaluating whether your assumptions and mental models are helping or hindering you.

Growth Mindset - Observe how these numbers grow:

$2 \times 1 = 2$

$2 \times 2 = 4$

$2 \times 4 = 8$

$2 \times 8 = 16$

$2 \times 16 = 32$

$2 \times 32 = 64$

$2 \times 64 = 128$

$2 \times 128 = 256$

$2 \times 256 = 512$

$2 \times 512 = 1,024$ (after 10 doublings)

$2 \times 1,024 = 2,048$

$2 \times 2,048 = 4,096$

$2 \times 4,096 = 8,192$

$2 \times 8,192 = 16,384$

$2 \times 16,384 = 32,768$

$2 \times 32,768 = 65,536$

$2 \times 65,536 = 131,072$

$2 \times 131,072 = 262,144$

$2 \times 262,144 = 524,288$

$2 \times 524,288 = \underline{\mathbf{1,048,576}}$ (after 20 doublings)

One (of anything) becomes a Thousand after only 10 doublings. One can grow into One Million in just 20 doublings.

As you can see, if we started with One Dollar and simply doubled it twenty times, we'd have $1,000,000. Ta Da! Now you know how to be a Millionaire.

Obviously, I understand it's not that easy. However, if you can learn how to multiply your money just once, you can do it again and again. No need to overcomplicate it. The best application of this mindset is within your marketing budget. Every marketing dollar should return at least 2 dollars back into your business, and preferably more like $4 to give you room to have profits to live on while still allowing the ad budget to double again and again.

This is a simple math problem, but in reality it's a not-so-simple problem to solve. Let me clarify (that is why you're reading this book, right?)

Business is a game of doubling. Its about finding a system that works, that is also scalable, and doubling your profit over and over again forever. Simple, right?

The not-so-simple problem: most methods that agents try to use to rev up their business simply don't work that well (like door knocking, open houses, etc). The things that do work usually aren't scalable, especially not as a solo agent. If you can only knock 100 doors today, you can't go knock 200 tomorrow.

So, my search for effective and scalable methods led me in a different direction than most of my competitors, and I'll teach you the scalable ads and processes throughout the next section of this book. These systems allowed me to simply replicate my initial successes on a larger and larger scale as I grew. My growth didn't take more time, just larger investments into my advertising budget as my profits grew.

You and I are not scalable. We're human, so we do have inherent limitations, specifically time, energy, and focus. This is why heavy outbound prospecting methods like cold calling have inherent limitations. Most people can't keep doing that activity long enough to make it work, and then there's physically no way to grow beyond the available hours in the day. Not only is it mentally draining, but you literally only have 16 hours per day you could devote to it. That's the maximum capacity. There's no way to double it again.

In order to grow quickly and sustainably, we need to employ lead generation methods that are truly scalable by utilizing effective advertising and automated follow-up systems. When you have an ad that works, you can scale it an almost unlimited number of times by simply raising the budget and expanding the audience. After much trial and error, I've discovered some very effective marketing strategies and lead magnets I'll share with you soon.

Another point to keep in mind: the time we devote to servicing our clients is not scalable, unless we employ technology and automations to help cut down the hours spent per client. The client experience and their real estate results cannot be allowed to suffer, which brings me to Service.

Service Mindset

I lived to serve my clients. I'd do whatever it took to get their goals accomplished (within reason.) I became known as something beyond the Full Service agent.

I would do extra research, create detailed marketing campaigns specifically for each client, even pressure wash their front porch if necessary.

I did whatever it took.

I've written contracts at midnight because of a tight deadline. I've shown houses all day long. I routinely pay for cleaners, landscaping, and stagers, not just photography.

Real Estate is a product, but being an Agent is providing a service. Never forget that your level of service, determines the clients' level of satisfaction.

Ford and Tesla both sell cars. They're judged on the quality of those products.

You sell a Real Estate Service. You're judged on the quality of your service.

The higher your level of service, the higher your word of mouth advertising will grow. And that's the best kind of advertising, because it's FREE!

When your clients are all raving fans, your business will absolutely explode. Most people think Cylinder #1: Lead Generation is the most important piece of you business engine, and it is until you have a lot of past clients, and then #6: Referrals will take over as the main driver of new business. It's like having a supercharger on your business, adding tons of free leads into the mix.

But that's only true if your service is impeccable. Otherwise, you'll be stuck with a subpar business, always relying on the Lead Generation cylinder, which is very expensive and time intensive.

So build a world class Service Model that your clients will rave about. Always be on the lookout for ways to improve it and add more value to your clients' lives. Continually ask, "How can I give them more? How can the process be smoother, faster, better?" It's a mindset that won't steer you wrong.

Habitual Mindset

Anything worth doing once is worth turning into a habit.

We are what we continually do.

Runners run. Musicians make music. Real Estate Agents do Real Estate deals.

If you aren't consistently working on one of the 6 Cylinders in your business on a daily or weekly basis, you're not really in the game. You aren't performing the actions that go with your job title.

Specifically, lead generating and following up should be done every day. Conversion appointments should take place every week. Closings should be happening every month.

If those things aren't happening, you aren't in the habit of practicing your craft. That's like a mechanic who refuses to turn a wrench, or a racer who doesn't drive any laps. You're guaranteeing your own failure.

So much of my success came from setting a weekly and daily schedule for all my major tasks, and never wavering from it. I structured my life around income generating activites (content & calls) and turned them into habits. And there were many other supporting habits that I needed to install in my life to stay consistent.

I had a specific wakeup schedule that started at 5 am. So, I woke up and knocked off at least one work task (blog post, video script, weekly email, etc) before Amanda and the kids were out of bed.

Everyday, from 9 am to 10:30 am, I called my current leads and pipeline of business to see how I could assist them.

I had a content schedule which told me every Tuesday I would be filming a new video ad and promoting it on Facebook.

Once a month, on the first Monday, I researched and wrote a Market Update blog article.

Those aren't necessarily the times you should do those things, or even the tasks you should do, but the point is that I established habits. Be intentional with your efforts, and put them on repeat. The schedule was set to repeat in Google calendar and it automatically filled my future, for unending weeks in advance.

And most importantly I stuck with it long enough for it to become a habit. Once a habit is set, you no longer have to think about it. It's just what you do <u>because it's Who You Are.</u>

Risk Mindset

> "I'll tell you what changed my whole life: I finally discovered that it's all risky. The minute you got born it got risky. If you think *trying* is risky, wait until they hand you the bill for *not trying*.
>
> **I'll tell you how risky life is. <u>You're not going to get out alive</u>.**"
>
> *– Jim Rohn*

Everything you try either works or it doesn't. If you crash and burn, just rebuild and do it a little different next time. Learn from your mistakes. Failing is actually part of the Success Process.

If it works, great! Now double it.

If it doesn't work, great! Try again.

If it still doesn't work, great! Try it again.

Eventually, you'll find what works. Great! Double it.

From the age of 12 to 15, I raced motocross bikes. I spent a lot of time ripping around our farm, and up & down the surrounding dirt roads. I also loved reading the magazines and watching videos of the pros flying through the air on their motorcycles, clocking frighteningly fast lap times. One of those pro riders at the time was a South African by the name of Greg Albertyn. He was having a tough season, and I remember reading an interview with him where he said:

"If you're not crashing, you're not racing hard enough."

– Albee

For whatever reason, that has stuck with me into adulthood. You never know your limits unless you exceed them every now and then.

So whether it was making a cold call or knocking on a stranger's door, I was always willing to risk failure to get the reward I wanted. Eventually, I did determine that traditional cold calling and door knocking were losing strategies for me because of the lack of scalability. But the key is that I wasn't afraid to try it.

I've also never been afraid to take on a client with a different type of property I've never sold. And I've never been afraid to try social media marketing, or to jump in front of a camera for video promotions. I've always just given an honest effort at every facet of this business I encountered. And that willingness to try in spite of potential failure has made all the difference.

To *try* is to risk failure, but *not to try* is to guarantee it.

Quite often, failure is simply a part of the success process. This point was driven home in the book *The Talent Code* by Daniel Coyle. In it, the author explores how true mastery is obtained in almost every human skill, from soccer to music, skateboarding to chess. The process of Deep Learning, as he calls it, is often quite painful. There are many unsuccessful attempts at the skill in the beginning, and then a tiny breakthrough, followed by more failed attempts, and then after much repetition a low level of proficiency develops. It often takes several years of these types of Deep Learning sessions for that proficiency to become mastery.

Failure is not just a part of the process, but it's *an essential* part of the process. Mastery cannot happen without multiple repetitions, and many, many failures along the way. It's how we learn. It physically rewires our brains to support the neural pathways that deliver the successful result.

In our profession, this process applies to all of our skill-based performance cylinders, specifically marketing, sales skills, and negotiating. The more you do them, the better you will be. For example, expect thousands of repetitions before your phone sales skills are master level. There will be many hang-ups and awkward conversations that make your heart race before you'll be able to easily book appointments over the phone.

See failures for what they are: building blocks to success.

Risk. Fail. Learn. Risk again. Fail. Learn. Risk. Succeed.

The risk is essential. The failures are essential. The success will come.

Principles

The following Ideas are thoughts I've come to live by. These principles helped mold my self-image into the identity I needed to have in order to find the success I so desired.

Principles help narrow and quicken your decision making capabilities. "I do *this action* because I have *that belief*. I do *this,* because I'm the type of person who does *that* type of thing.*"*

Some of these have become affirmations, which I repeatedly wrote down while writing my daily and weekly goals. Others are just observations, truths I've discovered along the way.

Try them out. See if they shift your perspectives on life the way they have shifted mine. If your perspective changes, your view of yourself might even change. And if your self-image changes, your identity changes. Then anything else in your life can change too.

Success is Scary, Hard, and Boring

I call this the **SHB Principle**. When we first try to learn a skill, we'll fail often. And that's **Scary**. We're all afraid of failure, and that inhibits our desire to master a skill.

In trying and failing, we discover that most skills worth having are difficult to master. They're **Hard**. Converting a lead into a client is hard. Negotiating a contract is hard. But this is a good thing. The harder a skill is to perform, the more valuable that skill is to the marketplace. The more of these skills you can acquire, the more income you'll receive.

And then, when you've finally mastered a skill, it becomes **Boring.** There comes a point where making calls to your inbound leads isn't Scary anymore, it's not Hard, it's just Boring. You won't want to do it.

At any stage of our development, the path forward is to continually perform the tasks we don't want to do. If it's **Scary, Hard, or Boring**, it's probably the right thing to be doing.

Successful people do the things their competitors aren't willing to do.

Think in Thousands

I asked myself a powerful question: "If I needed to land a listing client TODAY, how many people would I have to speak with to make it happen?"

Well, let's assume people move once every ten years. (The average is really something like seven or eight, but ten is a nice round number to start with.) So, if I talked to ten random homeowners, the odds are pretty good one of them would be moving this year.

But let's say I need someone to list this month, not just sometime this year. So now I need to multiply that 10 by the 12 months of the year. So 120 random conversations to find someone needing to list this month.

(For our purposes later in this exercise, rounding down to 100 will work pretty well, conceptually.)

Great! That seems doable. Just talk to about 100 people. But in reality, not everyone that needs my servie will use me to fulfill that need. There are almost 4,000 people with Real Estate licenses in my little market. That's a lot of competition.

Based on our agent count (~4,000), divided by our population size (~500,000), and then multiplied by 600 (the number of people the average person knows personally), I determined the number of agents the average resident knows personally. That number is about 5. The average homeowner in my area already knows about 5 Realtors®.

So in addition to the 5 they know already, there are several others that are advertising to them on a consistent basis. In their average day, that homeowner probably drives to work and hears a radio ad for a top ranked agent, then on their lunch break they scroll social media and see a few real estate ads as well. On their drive home, they pass a fancy billboard with a huge photo of an agent's smiling face. They check their mailbox and get a postcard for Real Estate services as well. And they get these marketing messages on a consistent basis.

So now, let's say that average homeowner has at least 9 options for Real Estate services rolling around in their head at any given time. My goal is to be #10.

So if I've got a 1 in 10 shot with any given homeowner, and they only need my service 1 out of every 100 months or so? **That means I need to be in front of at least 1000 homeowners to have a good statistical shot at booking a listing.** (10 competitors x 10 years x ~10 months = 1000 homeowner audience)

This why I decided to start <u>Thinking in Thousands</u>. If I want 2 listings per month, I need to be in front of at least 2,000 homeowners consistently. 4 listings = an audience of 4,000.

Now, the beauty of this scenario is that, within the same block of 1,000 homeowners, there will be another statistically good chance for landing a listing the next month as well. I don't necessarily need to go get a different thousand. I can keep marketing and communicating with the same group. And over time, with consistent messaging, my odds might even get better within that group.

Most agents aren't thinking this big. And their methods will never allow them to communicate consistently with a group this big. Cold calling and door knocking just aren't practical when the numbers get this large, at least not without months of effort.

Back to my original question "If I needed to land a client TODAY", it's just not practical to be in touch with that many people within one day's time. "One-to-one" communication is just too slow. I realized I would have to rely on "one-to-many" types of communication. I would need to advertise in order to hit my goals, not just rely on prospecting efforts.

Work Harder, Better, Faster, Smarter, Stronger, Longer than the Competition

Even though this might seem to contradict the lesson above, those with a huge work ethic stand out from their competitors. I'm inspired by stories of Kobe Bryant being in the gym at 3 am and getting 3 or 4 practices in every day. I also took note when Elon Musk stated that if your competition puts in 40 hours a week, while you put in 100, you'll accomplish the same goal in less than half the time.

And yes, I know it came from a Daft Punk song, but I felt the need to add "Smarter" and "Longer" to "Harder, Better,

Faster, Stronger." It became a powerful mantra in my head anytime I didn't want to put in the work.

Harder, Better, Faster, Smarter, Stronger, Longer!

I'd even ask myself things like, "How am I going to work **Harder** than other agents today? How can I provide a **Better** service? Can I provide **Faster** Follow Up? Can I come up with **Smarter** strategies to sell their homes for more money? Could I have a **Stronger** Marketing Message? Am I willing to work **Longer** than anybody else to accomplish my goals faster?"

HBFSSL! Outwork everyone.

Then when we take that intensity and apply it toward "one-to-many" marketing, we've got lighting in a bottle.

Think at least 3 Steps Ahead

Learn to play chess when others are playing checkers. Thinking multiple steps ahead allows you to see problems before they happen and build solutions before they're needed.

I literally did learn to play chess. I downloaded *Magnus Trainer* to my phone, which is a training app developed by the Grand Master and World Champion, Magnus Carlsen. I worked a few lessons into my morning routine. I quickly realized that the principles I learned could apply to real life as well.

For instance, in a good chess structure, the pieces all support each other, protecting each other from attack. It's like defense and offense at the same time. Business systems should be like that too. There should be no holes, just a strong, seamless process from beginning to end.

In chess, if you can think enough steps ahead, you can determine the outcome of a specific move before you even make it. This is especially true if you can force your opponent to make a certain move in response to your moves.

I've noticed that this concept of "forcing moves" is really handy as an agent. When negotiating a deal with another agent, I might make small asks or leading statements, already knowing the two most likely responses, and whichever one they give, in the end they're revealing more information that could help my client.

It's particularly important to "think ahead" to discover issues and problems before they arise. And if there are recurring problems that most clients run into, build a system around it. Later in the book, I'll teach you a system I built to answer most clients' listing objections before I even arrive to the listing appointment.

Likewise, it's a good idea to think several steps ahead and check for common inspection issues on homes you're about to list. Make sellers aware of what the inspector will likely flag as an issue, and prepare their responses before the buyer even makes the request.

Take Immediate Action (as soon as you know you should)

As important as thinking ahead is, if we don't take action we'll never get the result. And quick action always beats slow action.

This goes back to having the risk mindset as well. If we take action and it turns out to be a mistake, we can also quickly learn from the mistake and pivot to a new solution.

If we take an action, whether we're right or wrong, we're several steps ahead of where we were originally. We're winning either way.

It helps me to see each day as a race (even if it's only a race against the clock, and against myself, trying to get more done than the previous day). If I just sit at the starting line of a race, every second I wait to get started is another second I'm falling behind.

So, as soon as I think I know the right course of action, I jump on it immediately. No delay. **Take immediate action.**

This is especially helpful for things I don't want to do. I just realize that the longer I put it off, and the slower I go, the more misery I'm putting myself through. Better to get started immediately.

Immediately answer the phone when it rings. Immediately call that lead as soon as it comes through your systems. Crank out that piece of content you want to procrastinate on. **Take Immediate Action.**

It's Not About the House, It's About the People in the House

So often, I hear new agents say they got into the business "because I just love looking at houses." It's as if they're trying to turn their love of watching HGTV into their career choice. I think that's an unrealistic expectation.

The reality is that I spend a few hours per week going through nice homes with clients, but the majority of my time is spent at my desk working. I'm either creating content for people to consume, speaking with people about their housing goals, or making notes in the CRM (Client Relationship Management) software. I'm constantly trying to start and manage relationships with people.

The house is just a vehicle for people to experience the type of lifestyle they want to live. The business of Real Estate Agency is about serving people. Finding the house is just one aspect of that service.

I've also noticed that people only move to a new home when they really need to. It's always a life-changing event. It could be something as dramatic as a divorce or a death in the family, or it could be a relocation for work. Often, it's just time for a change due to their stage of life, as is the case when a family grows too large for the space they're currently living in, or when those kids move away to college and it's time to downsize.

In all these instances, the reason lies with the people, not the house itself. So, focusing on building great relationships with my clients has helped my business tremendously. When I dig deep to truly understand their needs, their problems, and their dream outcomes, it deepens the relationship, it improves my service, and the house just falls into place naturally.

Hit the Target: the 3 A's

Acquisition – Alignment – Accuracy

In the early part of the 2010's I got interested in a unique discipline of competitive shooting with the International Defensive Pistol Association. (I know, I know. As you can already tell by this point in the book, I'm interested in a weird mix of activites. I take inspiration from odd places sometimes.)

The practitioners of this sport train to hit targets as quickly as possible while still maintaining accuracy, which is a difficult endeavor to accomplish. If you've ever seen "behind the scenes" videos of Keanu Reeves training for his part in **John Wick**, that would give a pretty good sense of the intense style of firearms training I'm talking about.

It's really quite impressive to witness. When the timer goes off, the shooter punches the gun toward the first target, fires two shots **"Bang-Bang"**, whips the gun to another target with no hesitation, blasting another two rounds into that one as well **"Bang-Bang"**. Except there's no break in the rhythm between those two targets. So in real time it just sounds like **"Bang-Bang-Bang-Bang."** And then this unbroken staccato rhythm continues across 8 to 10 targets, with the only break in the banging occuring when the gun runs out bullets, and a magazine change is necessary. And even the magazine changes are done with piercing speed, routinely taking less than two seconds to complete. And then the **"Bang-Bang"**s start right up again.

Anyway, one of the absolute masters of the sport was Brian Enoch and he wrote a book called *Practical Shooting: Beyond Fundamentals* in which he explains:

> "Locate the target. Get the gun on the target. Keep the gun on the target while you fire the shot."
>
> – *Brian Enos*

Acquisition – Alignment – Accuracy

If ever I'm not hitting my goals, my targets in business, I break it down this way.

1. Am I sure of my target? Have I clearly defined my goal? Have I **Acquired** that clear image? If not, there's no way I'll hit it. In business, the goal equation should be something like: **I achieve X-Result by Y-Time**.

   (More on Goal Setting in Part 4 – Ignition: Starting Up)

2. Am I **Aligned** with that goal? Is my mind convinced? Do I really believe I can acheive it? Do I have the right strategy in place? Do I have all the systems and tools I'll need? Do I know what steps I should be taking on a day to day basis?

3. Am I staying **Accurate** to the goal? **Accuracy is taking action while maintaining alignment.** Am I staying true to the course of action I've laid out? Am I taking the necessary actions? Am I switching strategies instead of seeing it through to the end?

   (More on measuring your actions in Part 6: Gauges)

These **3 A's** are phenomenal for troubleshooting problems in my business. This methodology allows me to identify exactly where I'm falling off the goal, and exactly why I'm missing the target.

Every goal you achieve follows this exact process. **Acquire** the target. **Align** your systems with the target. Maintain that alignment while taking the necessary actions to hit the target. That's **Accuracy**.

Then you repeat the process for the next goal, and the next, and the next. Pretty soon you're blasting through targets like you're an action movie star!

"I'm a Positive Influence on Everyone I Meet"

This is an affirmation I've repeated to myself for years. I won't go into a lot of detail for this one because it is so simple.

Be nice. Smile a lot. Leave everyone better than you found them, no matter the circumstances. I try to live up to this one as often as I can.

"I Make Dreams Come True"

Another of my favorite affirmations. I strive to help others achieve their wildest dreams. Obviously this is great for clients, but I also try to apply it to friends and business partners as well.

How can I help this person achieve their highest aspirations? Do I have a connection they need to meet? Have I learned a lesson that applies to their situation? What can I give that will help their dreams come true?

Another beautiful aspect of this phrase is that if you help enough other people, you'll be helped in return. This Real Estate career has literally helped my family and I make our dreams come true as well.

The path to our dreams is in helping other people's dreams become reality first.

Part 2:
The Sales Engine

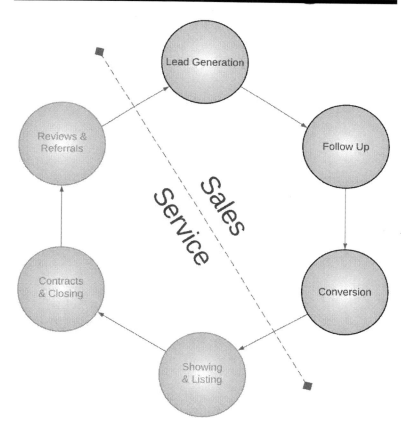

Your Business should be evenly divided between activities to gain new clients and activities to provide those clients with exceptional representation. In short, you have two sides of your Growth Engine: <u>Sales & Service</u>.

Cylinder #1: Lead Generation

Perhaps unsurprisingly, this will be the longest chapter of this book. Volumes have been written about this portion of the business. In fact, most of the training and coaching within the industry revolves exclusively around lead generation. If there's one thing all agents want more of, it's leads. I think of this Cylinder as my Marketing/Advertising/Branding Pillar.

When I first started in the business I found scores of gurus preaching their own "True path to success" through some proprietary lead generation method. There was the **"Cold Calling"** guru, the **"Door Knocking"** guru, the **"Open House"** guru, the **"For Sale By Owner"** guru, the **"Referral"** guru, and even the **"Writer/Blogger/Newsletter"** guru.

Now, I constantly see ads for the latest generation of Lead Gen experts, mostly teaching mastery of specific digital platforms: The **"YouTube/Video"** gurus, the **"Social Engagement"** gurus, the **"Facebook Ads"** gurus, etc.

I've read and watched content from most of them, and I learned a tremendous amount. However, I've come to believe there's no "One True Path" that every agent should follow.

Throughout my career, I've gotten business from all the methods mentioned above. They all work if you work them. All have their merits as well as their limitations.

I'll be sharing my best performing campaigns in this chapter, but by no means are these the only ways to bring leads into your business. This is an old business with many agents using countless strategies over all that time. Many old-school strategies are still viable, and I'm not here to bash other coaches or approaches. But I want you to focus on an approach that makes the biggest **impact**, that is **scalable**, and that allows you to **double your results over an over.** To that end I'll share a very powerful method here, and I'll tell you why it works for me.

Again, I'll reiterate that many other methods are viable. They all work to some degree **if you work them. However, don't get distracted by every option under the sun.** Here's just a handful of approaches that will be pitched to you: Circle Prospecting, Sphere-of-Influence prospecting, FSBOs, Expired/Withdrawn Listings, Divorce/Probate Attorneys, Door Knocking, Open Houses, Networking, Billboards, Bus Benches, Radio Ads, TV Ads, Newspapers/Magazines, Sponsorships, and the list goes on and on.

And this is the downfall of too many agents. They buy a course on some particular method, implement it halfway, get a handful of leads, get dissapointed that dollars & deals aren't just falling in their lap, and then they go buy another course. I know because I've done it. I fell into the trap of *Shiny Object Syndrome* which leads to *Information Overload.*

Don't do that. If you're just starting out, I want you to commit to mastering 1 or 2 lead generation methods MAX, preferably the ones I show you here, and purposely postpone all other methods until you've achieved mastery with it. You don't have time to learn it all, and you won't have enough energy to do it all. You just need one reliable method (or two max) to allow potential clients to raise their hand and alert you to help them.

That's the only point of this section: **to find someone who's never done business with you and move them into the next step, your Follow-Up funnel.** Don't let it overwhelm you.

To keep it simple, at the Lead Generation Stage there are three fundamental questions to consider:

- **Who am I serving?**
- **How do I communicate with them?**
- **What can I offer them that solves their problems?**

Who?

Generally, your leads will fall into one of two categories:

- People Who Find You
- People Who You Find

Most forms of **Advertising** are designed to allow people to find you. Old school techniques like Yellow Pages listings, TV/Radio Ads, Bus Benches & Billboards, etc. were all designed to allow strangers to become aware of you as a professional. The modern, digital equivalents of this are Google Adwords, your YouTube Channel, and Content on Social Media (both paid ads and organic posting.)

Most Forms of **Prospecting** are designed to allow you to go out and actively find people who might do business with you. This is what Door Knocking, Open Houses, and Cold Calling all accomplish for you. This allows you to define a certain group of people you'd like to serve, and then go speak with them directly.

The downside of traditional **marketing** is that it is very expensive. Conversely, traditional **prospecting** is very time intensive. **What if** I told you there was a way to marry the two ideas? **What if** this new way of doing things was cheaper to implement than traditional advertising, and saved countless hours over prospecting? **What if** you could deliver your message directly to the exact people you wanted to do business with, and only Follow Up with them when they show interest?

Well, that's the exact method that has worked wonders for me. I call it the **Alpha/Omega Strategy**. Once I implemented this strategy, I've never looked back.

Here's how it works:

- Define the exact neighborhoods you'd like to work.
- Use a data aggregator to collect all the homeowners' contact information.
- Use that list of homeowners to create a "custom audience" in Facebook Ads Manager. **(Omega List)**
- Deliver ads to that audience.
- Also send ads to a general audience to allow people to find you, thus growing your audiences over time. **(Alpha List)**
- Market to your core audience in as many ways and on as many platforms as possible.
- Only directly communicate (call, text, etc.) with the ones who reach out to you and become a lead.

This allows you to market to an audience you've clearly defined (prospects you choose) and also allows you to grow an interest based audience of people who find your content (prospects that choose you). Both strategies can be fulfilled on one platform in the beginning. Currently, I recommend the **Meta (Facebook) Ads Platform** due to the number of users and the low cost. To date, I haven't found another platform as capable as that one. I'm constantly on the lookout for better options, but I haven't found anything that competes with it yet, especially for the ability to define a **Custom Audience** and continually re-market to the same group over and over again.

Finding Your "Who"... The Omega List

Did anyone ever tell you that you can simply choose the main group of clients you do business with. You can simply declare, **"These are my clients. This is who I want to serve!"**

At the beginning of my career, I wish someone would have pointed this out to me. I was too busy chasing the next "Top-Secret" Hack to get my next lead that I:

- jumped from annoying the heck out of FSBOs
- *to* posting randomly on Social Media
- *to* knocking on the doors of that morning's Expired Listings
- *to* writing blog articles that nobody ever read
- *to* taking 2 hours on a Sunday morning and staking out 50 Open House signs just hoping a great lead would show up at the doorstep.

Yes, I was taking action, but I was waiting until the market, dumb luck, or the chaos of the universe just happened to deliver a client to me. I was essentially waiting for money to fall into my lap even as I anxiously ran around trying to find something that "clicked."

Nobody told me, "Colley, just pick your client base, and then go serve them." If someone had, I could have shaved years off my hardship. So, I'm telling you now: **"Pick the clients you want to serve. And never stop serving them."** This level of consistency is the best way to gain real traction in this career in both the short term and the long term.

So, let's discuss how we go about defining this initial list of prospects. For the purposes of a Real Estate Career, the easiest and most effective way is to start by researching the homes they own. By the way, I always try to prioritize homeowners because each lead has the potential bring two paychecks, one selling and one buying. Plus, it's harder to get a list of renters, although that's what you'd need to do if you wanted to serve first time homeowners with this method.

(By the way, remember the Fair Housing Act prevents housing discrimination based on race, color, religion, national origin, sex, disability, and familial status. Make sure you include everyone in the group you choose to market toward. This is why I focus on marketing to entire neighborhoods, and multiple neighborhoods at that.)

Let's make some decisions about your ideal business. **If you could only sell one type of home, what would it be?**

For instance:

- **In what areas or neighborhoods do you enjoy selling?** (Don't limit yourself to just the neighborhood you live in, although you might start there.)
- **What suburb or part of town do you know best?**
- **Do you prefer newer homes, or older homes?**

- **Do you prefer more expensive homes for the higher commission, or less expensive homes for the faster turnover?**
- **Is there a certain builder whose homes you absolutely adore?** You could target the neighborhoods they've previously built.

Write down all these criteria for yourself, and then go searching for the past sales that match that criteria in the MLS. Identify those neighborhoods that contain the bulk of your ideal property listings. These are the neighborhoods you should mine for data.

Notice that I said *neighborhoods* (plural), not just one ideal neighborhood. This strategy may initially look like the traditional "Neighborhood Farming" technique you may have heard about. That technique usually involves attempting to "own your neighborhood" by selecting a neighborhood of 300 to 500 homes and then making yourself known to that community. The typical recommendation is that you door knock these homes regularly, send postcards, mail a community newsletter, and hold neighborhood events.

This approach can certainly work, but the bottleneck on this strategy is the door knocking. I know from experience that door knocking is a huge time suck, even if you're meeting great people. However, the majority of the folks you run into aren't thrilled to see someone on their doorstep begging for business. Also, the contact rate is atrocious. Many people simply refuse to answer the door. Alternatively, they'll talk to you through their Ring doorbell and tell you "Not interested."

The other big downfall is that this approach leaves you thinking small. The advice to focus on one neighborhood is flawed in my view. Remember our principle: **Think in Thousands!** (pg. 29) a list of 300 to 500 homes simply isn't enough.

When I door knocked, I went broke, even though I went bigger than one neighborhood and knocked on 3,000 doors! It's because my contact rate was usually less than 20%, which means thousands of attempts only resulted in a few hundred touchpoints. Plus, it took months of unpaid hard work to accomplish. And I'd only gotten to each house **One Time!**

Even if we judge traditional farming by the postcard method, again in my experience, I need at least 1,000 people to be receiving postcards for at least 6 months to have good odds of getting a listing from that group. This is a good approach to employ once you have cashflow coming in and you can afford to commit to it long term. But starting out with it will just drain your bank account.

We need a better approach, a modern, supercharged strategy to revamp "Farming" for the current era.

All that being said, I recommend putting together a list of 10,000 to 20,000 "ideal addresses." I call this my **Omega List!**

For me, the Omega List is the Be-All End-All of my client base. I call them Omegas because once I have that list of homes, *that's the End of my hunt for leads.* (Aside from updating it every once in a while as inventory sells) **If I never did business with another client outside of this list, I'd be happy.**

For my Omega List, I've consciously decided that these are my clients, my people, the ones I choose to serve and solve problems for. I want to think about the market through their eyes, and craft solutions to all their pain points. This will help immensely when determining our **What?** (as in "What's the offer?" coming up later in this chapter)

I can hear you now, "I can't help 10,000 people at once, Colley! Are you insane?" I'm well aware that this sounds like an overwhelming number. Heck, there are only about 12,000 closings per year in my market. You'll never be able to take on that many people as clients. I know. But are you committed to serving them if given the chance? That's the question.

The reality is they won't all use you as their agent, even if you were optimally marketing to them with several touchpoints across multiple platforms *and* you personally called them once a quarter *and* you hand delivered a tin of Holiday Cookies every year with a personalized note written in calligraphy. THEY WON'T ALL USE YOU.

This is a numbers game, and unfortunately, the numbers required for success are very large. Your goal is to start with a large list, communicate with as many of them as possible, in the most efficient and effective possible form, and scale that communication over time to include every other form of communication with more and more touchpoints so that you are well known by all the members of your Omega List. And even then, only about 1 in 1,000 will use you for your services in any given month.

As your number of touchpoints grows over time with your lists, both Alpha and Omega, your corresponding number of deals from that list will grow as well. Repetition will be key, and your communication will become more and more effective as time goes on. At maximum capacity, signing 1 listing per 1,000 list members per month is very achievable. And then your business will crank out those results month in and month out, for as long as your communication (marketing) is consistent.

So how do we get this list of **Omega** homeowners?

That's the easiest part. In fact, I was shocked how easy it was to get the address, name, phone numbers, and email addresses for homeowners in my area.

Simply go to a company called RedX and buy their GeoLeads package. For a small monthly payment, I was able to pull 5,000 property records per month. It's so simple to map out a target neighborhood (which we've previously identified from the ideal homes we searched in the MLS) and have the data aggregator instantly deliver all the contact info with the click of a button.

Just go to www.LoneRockHomeTeam.com/AgentResources. Depending on promotional timelines, you might be able to lock in a discount through my link on that page.

So go pull that **Omega List** now, before we move on to the next client pool, **the Alpha List.**

"Who" Finding You... The Alpha List

The Alpha List is gained by being the Alpha Agent in your marketplace. I call it the Alpha List because you attract these prospects through the content you produce, becoming the most dominant, well-known agent in their minds. Your goal is to be the #1 top-of-mind agent for them: the Alpha.

These people have engaged with your ads, and will continue to see your face, read your name, and hear your voice for years to come. **These people will become your true fans, and you can truly consider them to be your "Audience."**

With every ad you run, the Alpha List will grow because new people will engage with your ads. There have been several times when my Alpha List grew by over 1,000 people over a weekend! After two years, my Alpha List had grown to over 25,000 people consistently seeing my content. That's twice as many people as the yearly number of transactions in my marketplace. It's 5% of the population in my area. And it continues to grow!

When I go out shopping, it's weird to know that 1 in 20 of the people surrounding me have probably seen my smiling face on their phone.

It often happens that people think they know me but can't quite remember why. "Did you go to school at …?" or "Where do I know you from?" At other times, people have a solid recognition. A server at Chili's once interrupted our meal and asked, "You're that Real Estate guy on Facebook, aren't you?" "Yep, that's me." "Oh, wow. That's so cool!" (If you're curious, they weren't in a position to buy at the time.)

These are all members of my Alpha List. And tens of thousands of them have seen my market reports, upcoming listings, and top tips to win in the real estate market.

And then, often enough, I get a call from someone I've never met, and they're ready to buy or sell property. They explain, "I see you everywhere. You're always on Facebook, and we've been getting your postcards. We're finally ready to take the next step. Can you help?"

And that, my friend, is an **Alpha-Omega Lead.**

57

(I'll go into a deep dive about how to create an Alpha list later in this chapter, once I explain the ads that generate the list.)

How?

How can we most effectively and efficiently communicate with thousands of people? What Methods work best?

After spending over $100,000 across various different advertising types, and after countless hours writing, photographing, and filming Real Estate content, let me make a suggestion. Keep it simple in the beginning.

Videos and Photos of properties are the easiest ways to get the attention from potential clients. Afterall, if they're looking to move, they're looking for a house. As nice and friendly as we may be, the truth is that the client wants a house, not an agent.

So, keep the initial ads about houses, not about you. You'll allow people to opt-in and become a lead (Name, Phone, Email) in exchange for more information about these houses.

How should we distribute these photos and videos of houses?

Again, keep it simple. My advice is to start with Facebook Ads. You'll be able to reliably distribute your content to a large portion of your Omega List almost instantly. And you'll be able to easily build an Alpha List over the coming months through inexpensive ads.

As your income grows, you can begin **The Game of Doubling** (Growth Mindset.) You can expand your reach with more ads to an ever-expanding Alpha List, and you can put more great content in front of the Omegas.

As you scale up, you should also begin to include postcards to a portion of your Omega List. Believe it or not, postcards have given me a great return on investment. They're not as good as Facebook's ROI, but they're better than most other types of ads I've paid for. They're phenomenal for branding and authority building, but they need a long runway with multiple touchpoints before you'll gain traction with them. After about 6 months of starting my postcard campaign to Omegas, they started to generate about 1 listing per month, per thousand recipients.

Eventually, you'll be able to double the postcard audience again and again until you're reaching the entire Omega List with a physical card in the mailbox at least 16 times per year.

Facebook and Postcards may prove to be all you'll ever need to focus on. The results from just those two can be incredible. However, if you want to expand into the latest & greatest trends from there, be my guest.

Who knows? A brand-new content platform could see a rise in popularity and become a dominant force at any time. There may even be a completely different technology we've never dreamed of that offers an incredible new approach. It's worth keeping an eye on all the new opportunities on the horizon.

But be careful. Too many agents waste tons of money on radio & TV ads (dying media), billboards, magazines, and all kinds of other traditional media that cost a ton of money, but don't offer anywhere near the audience connection you can build through the simple plan I'm presenting here. Also, don't spread yourself too thin, chasing the latest and greatest new methods, especially at first. You'll run out of time and energy with little results to show for it.

What?

What can we offer them that solves their problems?

The #1 lead generation tool of the real estate industry has always been, and always will be access to information about homes. From the days of the "MLS Book" which was physically printed and delivered to brokerages on a weekly basis, to newspaper classifieds, then online classified ads, to Zillow's exploits in "stealing the agent's listing data" and delivering it directly to the public, one fact remains: the consumer just wants to know which house they should buy.

What do they want to see? <u>Houses</u>. **This is the Single Tried and True fact in Real Estate.** Everything else is secondary.

So many agents (myself included) try to get fancy and offer some special program or promotion to get a flood of clients rolling in. I've never seen this work as well as simply offering to show them what homes are for sale. There are many gurus selling a "special marketing formula" to get your phone ringing off the hook with sellers ready to list and pre-approved buyers ready to sign for a mortgage. However, my experience has been very different from those promotional promises. My worst performing campaigns have always come when I steered away from the basics.

So let me lay out the basics:

1. Advertise Properties to get leads
2. Follow Up with those leads to see what they need
3. Help them get what they want (Buying or Selling)

That's it. Not very complicated. Just stick with the basics, especially when you're starting out. If you have a limited budget, just do what's been tried and true for decades. It works.

What Ads to Run

(Before we dig into the specifics, I must apologize slightly for the limitations of this format. This book is intended to be a compilation of systems and strategies, not a technical manual explaining "how to build Facebook ads" with every click-by-click action along the way. The best resource for learning Facebook ads may actually be Facebook's ad platform itself. The free courses they provide at:
www.facebook.com/business/learn/courses can answer almost all your technical questions. But in general, you will need a **Facebook Business Page** *and you will need to sign up for a* **Meta Ads Manager** *account.)*

The "Homes List" Ad

If I could only run one type of ad for the rest of my career, it would be a "Homes List" ad.

As mentioned earlier, at the time of this writing, the Facebook ads platform is the best performing, lowest cost, easiest platform to run these ads. However, at one time, newspaper classifieds were the norm. And into the future, there will probably be some new technological wave and a virtual reality, artificial intelligence platform that will take over as the next big thing. But the principle of delivering information about the available inventory of houses for sale will be an evergreen hook for this industry. I don't think it will ever die.

When someone is thinking of making a move, the problem that needs solving is that they don't know what house they'll be moving to. So, their mind is constantly thinking about finding the right house. That's what our ads should focus on initially.

Remember, they don't think they need an agent, but they know they need a house. They're not even thinking about an agent yet. They're just preoccupied with finding the right house.

My best performing Facebook ads have compilation photos of different houses and they say something like, "We have compiled a free list of homes here in the XYZ area under $300,000" (or whatever the **median sales price** is at the time.)

Then include a button that says, "Click here to get the full list." When they click the button, Facebook will auto fill a form with their name, phone number and email address and all they have to do is click "Submit." Then, we set it up so that information gets deposited into our client relationship management software.

They are instantly transported to an IDX page on our website where they can peruse the latest listings within that search criteria. Pretty simple. But it's also very effective.

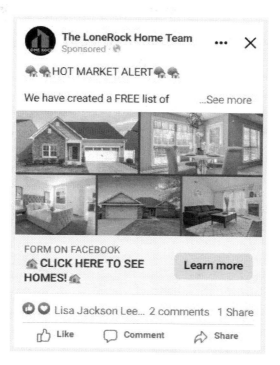

If you run this ad to a general audience on Facebook within a 15 to 20 mile radius of your target market you can generally get leads for only a few dollars apiece.

Of course, ad rates vary over time. But I've found that for about $10 per day Facebook will deliver two to four leads for me to follow up with. After doing this for a while, and because I have a strong automated follow up system, I'm able to convert about 1% to 2% of these leads in a given month.

Many people criticize Facebook leads as being weak leads because they feel that this is a poor conversion rate. And I'll show you how to increase the conversion rate shortly, but just realize that $300 to $500 in leads routinely generates two closings for me which can equate to $10,000 to $15,000 in commission in my market.

When you look at that return it's a 3,000% return on your investment. Where else can you get that kind of bang for your buck? Yes, you will have to call these people. Yes, there will be wrong numbers. Yes, some of them only want to rent and not to buy. Yes, some of them will speak a language you don't understand, and not all of them will want to use you as their agent.

But don't discount the fact that with a little hard work you can turn a $10/day ad into a $10,000+/month income quite simply and very quickly (within the first 3-6 months).

I like this ad because it's evergreen. You don't have to change the ad copy, and it works in almost any market. You'll just need to change out the image every couple of weeks. That refreshes the ad for the audience and you'll see more leads starting to come in again. These ads do get stale over time, so you have to freshen them up every once in a while with a new photo collage.

The "Direct Listing" Ad

The next ad I would run is a similar version of that "Homes List" Ad, but for a specific listing. This ad works off the same "show me the houses" principle as the Homes List. It's tried and true.

I post a select few pictures of that listing along with a short description and then say "For price and location, Click Here." Of course, that opens a lead form they fill out and then it directs them to your website to see the full House Listing.

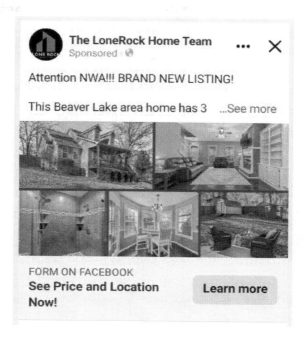

This one is great if you have a current listing or if someone else in your brokerage will allow you to run an ad for their listing. You may find buyers who are excited about that particular property and want to book a showing right then and there.

These leads often close at a slightly higher ratio than the generic homes list ads. I'd say it's more like 3% to 5%. Plus, your home seller will be ecstatic when you tell them the number of leads that are coming in.

This is a great tool for your listing presentation as well. You can share past results of these campaigns with potential listing clients. The only downside is that every time you sell a house, you have to pull a top performing ad!

Building the Alpha List

Speaking of listings, my favorite way of building a list of potential buyers who are excited about homes **(the Alpha List)** is to create video tours of properties. When done correctly, your Alpha List is an exponentially growing, retargeted, local audience. Here's how you do it.

Every time I take a listing, I make sure not just to get photos, but to have a professional video shot as well. I heavily promote that piece of content out to a ton of people in my local area. I believe we, the agents, shouldn't appear in the beginning of the video. Keep it about the house at first. The first 10 seconds should be the drone shots coming down the street, coming up the driveway, and giving a cinematic look at the house. This will probably be 2 to 3 shots of the exterior.

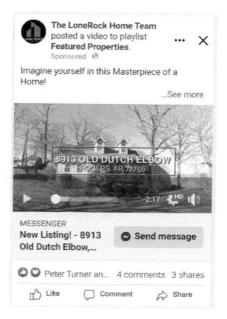

At 10 seconds into the video, I show up on screen to introduce the house. "Hello Northwest Arkansas, this is Colley Bailey with Fathom Realty, this amazing home has..." I give a brief blurb about the house which lasts maybe 15 seconds at the most, and then, "Come check it out with me!" And then the footage cuts to the interior walkthrough of the home. You could add a voiceover explanation of the rooms and features, but I generally don't in mine.

Then take this video and pump it out to the public with a **Reach Campaign Objective**, which is designed to get as much exposure as possible. Let's say Facebook gets it out to 50,000 people. In my area, for about $100 to $150, I can get it in front of about 50,000 people. I incorporate this cost into my marketing package for my listings. Just like I pay for a photographer, when that listing sells, it's going to pay me back for this ad.

Let's say, 1,000 people watch the first 15 seconds of it. Okay, well on Facebook 15 seconds is an eternity, right? People are generally swiping and scrolling in split second increments, unless something catches their eye, something they're actually interested in.

The majority of the 50,000 people that see it simply keep scrolling. They swipe it away. But, maybe 1,000 people, think, "Ooh! That looks nice. I've been thinking about moving. Let me keep watching." Those people are interested.

Facebook is storing that data for you. It keeps track of the accounts, this audience, that watched 15 seconds or more of your video. Now, you can create a **Custom Audience** of the people who watched a **"Thruplay"** (which is 15 seconds) in Facebook. So now you have an audience of 1,000 people that you can send other content back to in the future. Every time you have a listing, you can add to that audience and it will grow over time.

This Thruplay audience will become the backbone of your Alpha List. These are people who are interested enough to watch 10 seconds of a house and didn't scroll away as soon as they saw you, staying engaged for at least another 5 seconds. **You know two important things about this audience:** they're <u>interested in houses,</u> and they <u>know who you are</u>.

These are the people that would be most likely to look at future content. And we're going to re-target them and continue to grow that audience. I try to grow mine every month. Over the last few years, my Alpha List has grown to over 25,000 people. These people have seen tons of my ads at this point, and I make sure to put every new video or post in front of them first with a Reach ad targeted specifically to my Alpha List.

"But, I'm a Listing Agent"

I can hear it now. "But Colley, I want Listings! These are Buyer lead strategies. I want to get more listings and stop dealing with so many buyers."

While I agree that your business should be driven by Listings, I don't agree that there's a better way to get them than the fundamentals we've already discussed. I spent tens of thousands of dollars trying to crack the code of "Listing Leads," and the results were atrocious. I tried all kinds of promos from **"How to Sell Your House for More!"** PDF lead magnets to **"What's Your Home Worth?"** ads. I even created an entire **"Pre-Listing Price Accelerator" Video Program** to help Sellers boost their sale prices through better Preparation and Promotion. The goal was always to get Sellers to enter their info and become a

"Listing Lead." None of those direct response type strategies were worth the ridiculous ad budgets I spent on them.

(Luckily, I was able to repackage the Price Accelerator as a powerful Follow-Up and Conversion tool, but it's still not a great lead generator.)

And the truth is, I was just moving too far from the fundamentals. When a current homeowner is thinking of making a big life change, do you think they start by calling a home stager and running financial analysis of what their home is worth?

No! They do what the fundamentals indicate: they start looking for info about houses! If their house is too small, they look at bigger houses. If it's too big, they look at small houses. If it's too old, they look at newer houses. If it's in the wrong school district, they look for homes in a better school district. Too far from work? They look for houses closer to their employer.

They start as BUYERS!

When we take on clients, we're usually taking them on as buyers first, and listings second. We have to craft a workable transition for them. It's a huge life change, and a big problem for us to help them solve.

So, the goal should not be to avoid buyers, but to find buyers who also have a house to sell. Now they're both Buyers and Sellers. And our work will be rewarded with two commission opportunities instead of just one.

Enter: **the Omega List!** Remember that huge list of homeowners we made earlier? Well, this is exactly why we made that list.

We can use a targeted Homes List ad directly to those homeowners. And now when a lead comes through, we know that they also **most likely have a home to sell** in addition to whatever home they're looking for. **Buyer first, Seller second!** My favorites for this are Homes Lists that address common reasons for moving.

House too small? What about a Bigger Homes List?

House too old? What about a New Construction Homes List?

Ready for the Dream House? What about a Luxury Homes List?

I'm sure you can think of plenty of other specialized lists for your area and demographics. Get creative, but make it about the houses.

Here's a great ad example:

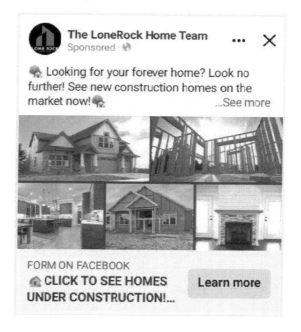

Be aware, these leads will have a higher average cost than if it were sent to a general audience. Maybe even 10 times the cost per lead. However, you're paying for efficiency here. Instead of needing to dial through 100 leads to find someone ready to do business, you're whittling them down to people who have a high likelihood of ownership and are also looking to buy. This will be a high potency lead. Treat them like Gold!

Creating the Facebook Omega List

Let's build that Omega List as a **Custom Audience** in Facebook. Once you've exported the list of potential homeowners from your target neighborhoods from the data aggregator, you can now upload those into Facebook's ad platform.

This will be another type of "Custom Audience" within the Facebook Ads Manager. The platform calls it a **Customer List audience**. You just need to make sure to format the list in an Excel spreadsheet to match Facebook's input algorithm. This just involves changing the column headers and deleting the unnecessary columns of the exported document.

Then you upload it into the Ads Manager and Facebook tries to identify the names, the phone numbers, and email addresses you've provided and cross references them with active Facebook profiles in their database.

In my experience Facebook found between 50 and 60% of an uploaded list from my Omega addresses. Yes, that's a pretty big drop in the data, but realize that not everyone is on Facebook. And the algorithm can't always match every profile to the data you've uploaded.

Again, this is why we **Think in Thousands**! If we've had a list of 10,000 people whittled down to 5,000 Facebook accounts, that's still a huge audience to start your career with. Wouldn't you say?

Again, these people will become the core of your advertising audience and we will make sure they (and the Alphas) see almost every piece of content we create over the coming months and years. They will become familiar with you and the solutions you provide. And when they think of Real Estate, you'll always be top of mind.

Top Video Ads

When it comes to which content to put in front of your Alpha and Omega audiences, I recommend various types of video content whole-heartedly. The goals with Video are branding, name recognition, familiarity, and authority building. This is not "direct response" marketing, but rather the goal is to become the most well-known agent or team in your area. Educating and entertaining your audiences will burn your brand into their subconscious. When it's time to buy or sell, you'll be the one they come to. This can also be thought of as a type of preliminary, automated Follow-Up (which we'll dig into in the next chapter.)

I would recommend creating the following types of content:

1. Testimonials and Case Studies

If you get a great review, make a video out of it.

Either the client can be on video if they're comfortable with that, or you can simply take a screenshot of the Google review and read it aloud. Then tell the story of have of the clients' journey in your own words.

Also, if you have a seller who goes all out with property preparation, you can take video of the rooms they're repainting and the pressure washer going across the driveway. Then, when the professional stager is there, get shots of that. At the end, compile all of that into the story of how they prepared their house and how they got a superior result in the marketplace.

I had one of those ads that did very well for me and is still something I share with potential sellers even in the middle of a listing presentation. I'll just pull it up on my phone and have them watch the 90 seconds. My value is clearly established.

2. Pro Tips

These could be:

- Top three ways to increase curb appeal.
- Top seven mistakes sellers make when putting their house on the market
- The biggest influences on your credit, things like that.

The point here is to establish credibility and professionalism. My honest advice to create content topics is to follow several top agents in various other markets around the country, watch their content, and then make something similar with your own spin on it.

These can be formatted like 2-10 minute "How to" type content that you might see on YouTube, or it could be more like a quick bullet point version for Reels or TikTok under a minute long. In addition to running these on paid Facebook ads, I also recommend putting the videos you create on all the different platforms to grow your organic audiences.

3. Market Updates

These can be short recaps of market activity, or they can be long in depth discussions with charts and graphs where you give predictions of what you see coming in the future.

These have been a mainstay for me, with many people seeing me as "the numbers guy" in my local community. Be careful with going too deep into the weeds in these videos. When reviewing backend metrics, you'll notice the watch times aren't usually that long for these videos. However, they do establish you as an expert in your field, so they're worth doing.

4. Neighborhood Features

What if you featured the neighborhoods your Omegas actually live in? Wouldn't that be surprising for them to see that you know their 'hood in so much detail? You can discuss when it was built, number of homes in the community, school districts, average number of homes that come up for sale every year, etc. This in depth data is something people are often curious about, but never have access to.

5. Community Spotlights

Show what's great about your city or region! These videos could feature:

- a park
- an event
- a small business
- a library
- a museum

- a city waterpark
- a golf course
- a lake
- a hiking trail
- a festival

These help break up the monotony of real estate content and help your audience learn more about the community, thereby making you an expert on the area. You can get really creative with these.

6. Area Information

What general info about your area can you bring to light? Things like:

- Moving to XYZ area? Here's what you need to know.
- What's it like to Live In XYZ?
- How Much House can $500,000 buy you in XYZ?
- Top 10 Things I love about XYZ
- Pros and Cons of Living in XYZ

This type of content does really well on YouTube and search portals, but it's also great for your Facebook audiences. Again, it builds expertise and authority on your area. Plus, they're a lot of fun.

General Observations on the Application of Fundamentals

You might have noticed a theme with the content in these ads. It goes back to that fundamental, "What do they want to see? Houses." Obviously, a **Direct Listing Ad** (photo or video) follows that advice, as it shows a single home for sale. **Homes List Ads,** follow this basic premise as well.

However, you might have missed the fact that the **Neighborhood Feature** is just an expanded way of giving information about houses (through their surrounding neighborhood.) **Community Spotlights** perform a similar function, explaining some of the fun features someone might enjoy if they lived in a certain area. Then the **Area Info** videos expand that concept out a little further.

Similarly, **Case Studies** tell the story of a particular family and their house. **Pro Tips** give helpful information about how the viewer can get their own house easier, with less hassle, and fewer issues. And of course, **Market Updates** are about the local housing market, comprised of all the houses being bought and sold.

Your marketing can stay centered around the house, and all the surrounding information. It works because that's what the Buyers and Sellers want to know. So, let's give them what they want in a way that separates you from all your competition. They can't get your exact perspectives from anybody but you, and not even Zillow can compete with you on that.

If you feel like you need help with Facebook Ads, I highly recommend working with Witly. They've been a game changer for my business. Anytime I need to get an ad up and running I email my account manager at Witly, upload the content and they build the ad, publish it, and send the leads directly to my CRM as soon as they come in.

Just go to www.LoneRockHomeTeam.com/AgentResources for a special deal with Witly through my link.

Postcards to Omegas

You might be surprised to learn that I recommend postcards even though we live in this fast paced, digital world. But high-quality, full-color physical print media provides something the digital experience can't. It makes you and your brand feel real. It exists in the real world, not just on a screen. It makes your business feel far more legitimate, and it presents you as a far more credible professional.

It takes a while to establish your brand with the recipients, but once you've been showing up in their mailboxes for about 4-6 months, you'll start to get those "Come List Me!" calls. It works. This is a tried-and-true traditional method which lets your Omega List know that you're active in the market and you can get the job done.

As for what marketing messages to put on the cards? I recommend keeping with the fundamentals like the video content above. With the caveat that you can display more information about your listing prowess. In fact, the back of my cards always has information about my listing packages and track record.

Here are some topic ideas:

1. Homes Lists

Direct them to your website, where they can login to see the list you've created for them. Again, always go back to basics.

2. Just Sold

This is the classic Real Estate postcard. Most people send these to the nearest 100-200 addresses around a recent listing, but I send them to my entire Omega List (or at least as many as I can afford to send to.)

3. Quarterly Updates

The next one I would highly recommend are Quarterly Updates with charts and graphs on the card showing market movement across your area. Maybe even breaking it down to average price per square foot across the different suburbs or towns that you service.

4. Testimonials

Much like the testimonial video on Facebook, these can tell the story of how a seller got a great result. It could be a Copy-and-Paste of great Google reviews from your clients with pictures of the houses you to worked on. An advanced "Just Sold" card.

5. Promotional Offer

Could you provide a free home warranty? If so, make it a promo!

Do you provide off market home searches where you will prospect specific neighborhoods to find the perfect home for your buyers even if it's not currently listed in the market? Make it a promo!

I've heard of an agent offering to pay for movers when a clients buys and sells with them. That makes a great "Free Mover" promotion.

Likewise, the "Sold in 30 Days or We'll Buy It" promotion is a very powerful one. Most agents using this one are partnering with a local cash investor and negotiating the discounted "we'll buy it" price upfront before listing.

Postcard Wrap Up

I recommend you start your postcard campaigns with a narrow slice of your full Omega List, preferably 1,000-1,250 addresses. Make sure you have enough budgeted to complete a 6 to 9 month campaign with them. Doing less than this number of addresses and less than this length of time is not likely to be effective.

They need to see your consistency. The repetition is the biggest key to success with this form of marketing. And postcards should be paired with a strong social media presence and video content.

As time goes on, just as your Alpha List grows on Social Media, your Omega Mailing List can grow as your listings and sales provide more of a marketing budget for future cards. I recommend growing from 1,250 to 2,500, then to 5,000, and eventually up to your total Omega List, maintaining a mailing volume of 10,000 or more.

I recommend maintaining at least 16 mailings per year, consisting of 12 monthly mailings and 4 quarterly (Market Update) mailings. You can always do more if you have a special promo, holiday, or event you'd like to share with your list. It is also highly recommended that you initially "seed" your list by sending 2-3 cards per month for the first three months of bringing in a new segment of your list.

From my experience, this should result in about 1 listing per 1,000 addresses per month. Mine started coming in at around month 3. And these have been "Come List Me!" type calls for me. The best type of clients to bring on, for sure.

Another big tip is to incorporate QR codes to easily allow the viewer to get more information on your website, especially video content. This can go to a squeeze page with a lead form, generating a lead for you to follow up with. Or just send them directly to the information, but use an advanced postcard printing company that can **autogenerate unique QR codes for each piece of mail which is matched to the address** it was sent to. Now you can find that lead in your Omega database and give them a Follow-Up call directly or mail them more detailed information about your services.

If you'd like to use the same printer I've been using, get in touch with PostCard Mania. They not only print the highest quality and most technologically integrated cards, but they can design them for you too. Every member of the staff has been a joy to work with. Just go to www.LoneRockHomeTeam.com/AgentResources , and I've worked out a special deal with PostCard Mania for readers of this book. You'll **save 10% on Design and Printing** through my link on that page.

Lead Generation Summary

In summary, I highly recommend you pick an audience of people you want to serve, several neighborhoods worth of homes that you are committed to helping, and continue to market consistently to them for years to come. This is your Omega List, your Be-All End-All client base. To begin with, I recommend starting with paid Facebook ads so that you can maintain precise control over who sees your content.

You can also build a base of other viewers who show interest in homes, your Alpha List, on the same Facebook Ads platform. Allow them, both Alpha and Omega, to opt in to get more information about homes in your area. Then Follow-Up with them to continue the conversation and serve their needs.

As you close more deals, engage in the Game of Doubling (Growth Mindset) and double your ad spend. Eventually, your efforts will allow you to start marketing postcards in their mailboxes as well. Again, grow that mailing list over time as more deals close.

There are countless other platforms and media you can advertise with, but these two have proven to be the most consistent and productive for me in my business. They allow me to bring in a predictable number of leads on a monthly basis. That consistency helps smooth out the rollercoaster of business so many agents find themselves on. I believe these are the best advertising spend to get established with, and then you're free to grow other methods over time.

Let's Rev it Up!!!

Next Steps:

1. Brainstorm Who your core audience will be, your Omega List. Do the research to determine what neighborhoods or niche you will serve.
2. Pull those contacts from a data aggregator like Red X.
3. Do you have a Facebook Business Page and Ad Account? If not, create those now.
4. Do you have a Homes List Ad running? If not, let's get one going now.
5. Brainstorm some video content types you can commit to creating and advertising on a weekly/monthly basis. Make a content calendar for the next year and time block it in your Google Calendar.
6. Define the first 1,000 addresses you will send postcards to when your budget allows.

Cylinder #2: Follow Up

Lead Generation is the flashy sportscar of the Real Estate business world. Everyone loves to hear about it, and every coach and guru loves to talk about it. But, Follow-Up is the work truck. It's the unseen driver of success, not getting near enough credit or near enough love. "How to get leads" is a much more popular topic than "How to Follow Up with leads" for good reason.

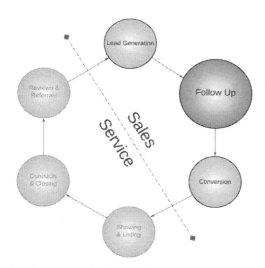

Follow-Up is Scary, Hard, and Boring. No other Cylinder of your business embodies that **SHB Principle** more than the Follow Up stage.

When agents are first told they need to call their leads, they are often panic stricken with fear. It's terrifying to call a stranger and try to do business with them. "What will they think?" "What if they hate me?" "What if they hang up on me?"

The mind immediately begins all the mental gymnastics necessary to avoid taking the necessary actions. "I should check my email really quick." "I wonder if anyone has commented on my Facebook post yet." On and on, the mind will stall, avoid, and run away from simply calling the lead. And the anxiety grows bigger and stronger.

To avoid all that drama, it's imperative that you simply make the call as soon as possible. Otherwise, the negative emotions will grow into a menacing monster in your mind. Yes, making the call is **Scary.**

However, once you get over the fear of that first dial, you'll feel more comfortable making the next one, and the next one. You'll probably start to get in a rhythm with your calls and start speaking with more and more prospects as your list of generated leads grows. Then you'll notice how difficult it is. **It's Hard!**

It's **hard** to get them to answer the phone in the first place (most won't.) It's **hard** to keep them on the phone and engaged in the conversation (most will try to hang up very quickly.) It's **hard** to get them to open up and share their situation with you, giving you an opportunity to help them. It will require skill and tenacity to connect with people deeply enough for them to trust you.

But it's necessary. You don't have a business if you don't have clients, and you'll never have clients unless you talk to the people who respond to your ads. Getting over the fear and the difficulty involved in Follow Up is critical.

And finally, once you've done thousands of dials, had hundreds of conversations, and helped dozens of clients, it will dawn on you: You're no longer scared to make the calls. You've developed the skill to convert those calls into appointments and appointments into clients. You're good at what you do.

But then the last stage sets in: it's **Boring**. You've been there and done that. It's a slog, a repetitive task that drains your energy and bogs you down. Your mind wants you to move on to something more entertaining, to stop making the calls and doing the daily drudgery.

Make no mistake, **Follow Up is the most difficult part of this career,** and its all because of this **SHB Principle**. And that's exactly why you should be thrilled to do it. If it was easy, fun, and carefree, everybody would be able to be a successful real estate agent and you'd never be able to compete. The fact that it is so Scary, Hard, and Boring for so many of us means it is the Ultimate Opportunity.

The agents who have the most conversations win. The ones who can't get themselves to reach out to their leads, go out of business. It really all comes down to your ability to embrace the difficulty and excel at the task anyway. It's your way to outpace the competition and hit the accelerator toward your dreams.

Levels of Communication

What makes for good communication? How should we reach out, and how do we make ourselves more effective?

The good news is that if you've fully implemented the Alpha/Omega strategy, your leads will know who you are before you call them. They may have been seeing your content for months now. Or maybe you're trying to follow up with new leads that just saw the Homes List ad with no other contact with your brand.

No matter how the lead came to you, let's explore the most effective strategies for communicating with them, from beginning to end:

Conversations (Active Communication)

The main goal is always to have an active conversation with these prospects. The first communication is probably just a quick back and forth that is going to lead to setting an appointment to go deeper into their situation. After all, you probably just called them seemingly out-of-the-blue. They may not have time for a lengthy discussion at the moment. To be respectful of their time, it's usually best to offer an appointment for a later time.

I like to call that appointment a Strategy Session, and I offer it as a free benefit to them which can improve their lives. It's purpose is to help them understand all their options and map out their next steps. Ultimately, that's the purpose of our **Conversion Cylinder**.

The purpose of our **Follow Up Cylinder** is simply to get them to book that **Strategy Session**, either a Buyer Consultation, Listing Consultation, or both.

When communicating with leads, here are **the Levels of Effectiveness in order:**

1. **In Person Meetings**
2. **Video Chats (Zoom, FaceTime, etc.)**
3. **Phone Calls**
4. **Typed Conversation (Text, Messenger, Email, etc.)**

So let's look at each of these in order of Effectiveness.

First, communicating with someone **In Person** will always be most effective. It instantly conveys familiarity and trust is more easily transferred. You have full use of body language, and this form of communication is where true salespeople shine.

Obviously, this is our most preferred situation and is why we'll try to get an In Person Strategy Session whenever possible.

However, our initial Follow Up to an online lead will almost never be In Person. We'll usually rely on other methods initially.

Secondly, **Video Chats** are the next best thing to In Person communication. If we can't physically be in the same room with someone, video is a great alternative. You can still see body language. You can hear intonation in the voice. And facial expressions can convey a lot of information.

Of course, we can't just jump to a video chat with someone who came to us as an online lead either. We need another form of communication to get us to the **In Person** meeting or the **Video Chat.**

That form of communication is a **Phone Call.** When speaking on the phone, yes, we lose facial expressions and body language. But it's amazing how much can be communicated simply through the tone of voice, the speed of delivery, and the confident communication of an expert salesperson.

This is why making the calls is of primary importance in our business. It's often the first line of communication that is effective enough to move someone to the next stage. But it's also distant enough that a good portion of population will engage.

Always, always, always lead with a Phone Call first, and then move to subsequent types of conversation attempts when following up with your prospects.

After phone calls, the next best type of communication is a **Typed Conversation.** Primarily texting, as it's the platform with the highest answer rate. People tend to respond to text messages more frequently than answering the phone.

However, it's harder to keep them engaged in the conversation. That conversation can go cold at any time. With no body language, facial expressions, or tone of voice, much of your communication is lost when texting. However, with good, well thought out questions you can often engage leads in a conversation that is productive.

Other types of typed conversations could also include Facebook Messenger, and email threads. In any case, the goal of a typed conversation should be to move the conversation into a phone call, and from there at video or in person chat.

Observation (Passive Communication)

Try as we might, some prospects will simply not engage in our attempts to communicate with them directly. They won't answer the phone and they may ignore text messages as well. If that's the case, the following forms of communication should be implemented:

1. **Personal Video** (Text, Messenger, Email, etc)
2. **Video Content** (Ads, Social, Search, Email, etc)
3. **Voicemail**
4. **Typed Conversation Attempts** (Text, Messenger, Email, etc.)
5. **Hand Written Letter**
6. **Branded Physical Marketing** (Postcards, Magazine Ads, etc)

If a prospect doesn't answer the phone after several attempts across a few days and your texts go unanswered, I highly recommend making a quick **Personal Video** introducing yourself. Call the prospect by name, point out their request for information, and that you're just following up to see how you can help. This humanizes you, and will often get a response when nothing else will. Text or email it to them.

The next most effective form of communication is **Video Content**. Of course, this is already occurring with the ads you're running on Facebook and other social media. You can also deliver helpful YouTube videos directly to them via text or email.

These videos should be helpful pieces of content that address their concerns, ease their fears, and help them achieve their goals.

Of course, after a phone call attempt, you can leave a **Voicemail** but in my experience many people don't respond as well to voicemail as they do some form of video content. So make sure to prioritize video in addition to leaving simple voicemails.

Even if people don't respond to early **Typed Conversation Attempts** through text or email, it's a good practice to continue attempting to contact them in this way. It gives them the option of responding on their own time, but reminds them you're there for them. I had some clients respond after my seventh text, leading to a lunch meeting and then very quickly to buying a house. That couple are now a very dear friends of mine.

Another visual form of communication is a **Handwritten Letter.** Of course, this is a true one way conversation. They won't be able to respond easily, but it's seen as a very heartfelt and genuine form of communication. This is helpful when trying to get a response from a prospect.

It's also important to remember this throughout your transactions with clients. At every major step, a nice handwritten letter or card deepens the relationship. This applies even after the sale. A handwritten request for a great Google review or a referral from a past client may be one of the most impactful uses of this strategy.

Don't discount all your **Branded Physical Marketing**; your postcards, brochures, magazines, presentation packets, etc. All of these help cement your value as an agent and your benefit to the client.

Phone Call Tips

I won't share a complete script with you here just for the sake of brevity, but I do think you should script out how you want these conversations to go and keep them short, light and to the point. My team uses a script I've developed, and I believe everyone should create their own scripting to build a genuine connection with prospects. In this section, I'll share the key components for you to consider.

<u>The first few seconds of the interaction are the most critical.</u> Your tone of voice must be confident and friendly. You must come across as if they are receiving a call from their best friend, not a telemarketer. This largely has to do with the intention that you've set with yourself. Before the call even begins, your attitude needs to be one of curiosity about their situation and be an attempt to serve them. You must want to be of help.

You should smile as you speak. They'll be able to hear the difference. If you are smiling, your voice sounds inviting and optimistic, as if you're excited to be speaking with them. That's the right tone. It has an energy that will distinguish you from telemarketers and spam callers.

When I call, I typically open the call by using their first name as a question "**John?**" and then quickly say, "**Hey, this is Colley... Here in Bentonville ... with Fathom Realty... How-you-doin'-today?**"

So, let's break that down. The first sentence that I say is broken up into three parts:

1. **My name** with an upward inflection (almost ending as a question),

2. Then "**here in** _____" (the town that I'm calling from), which should be local to the town they live in. That's very important, as it establishes a quick connection with them. Again, the voice inflection goes up at the end, not down. It ends almost as an upbeat question.

3. And then "**at Fathom Realty,**" my brokerage company. Again, Up. Question.

I give a slight pause in between each of those. Just enough for them to reflect. I want them to catch each piece of this information.

The phrase "**How you doing today?**" should all be run together almost as one word. It should be tagged onto the end of your introductory sentence with no room for interruption in between. No pause before you say it.

"..with Fathom Realty?->How-you-doin'-today?"

This should have a downward inflection to drive the point home and make an impact. Now you can pause to let them answer.

Visually, it might all be best represented like this:

John? This is Colley? Here in Bentonville? With Fathom Realty? How-you-doin'-today?

Say it as if you're trying to jog their memory. You should say it in a way that sounds like they should already know who you are (even if they don't). Like you're just returning a call that they've made to you earlier. Again, It should sound like they're already familiar with you and you're just trying to jog their memory. At each pause, their brain should be trying to recall who you are.

They should be thinking, "Oh, his name is Colley. How do I know Colley again?"

And then, while they're thinking that, they hear the next phrase. "Oh, in Bentonville. I live in Bentonville too. So I should know this person, right?"

And then while they're pondering this piece, they're hearing the next phrase. "Oh, at Fathom Realty. Oh ok, they're that agent I've been seeing on social media." It might click at this point, or it might not.

And then we put the ball in their court with "How-you-doin'-today?"

This first five seconds is critical.

If you sound like a telemarketer: **Click!** They will hang up.

If you sound weak: **Click!**

If you sound downbeat: **Click!**

If you sound too forceful: **Click!**

Again, the tone is friendly and helpful. There should actually be a smile on your face. You should go into the call thinking they're a good friend you haven't spoken to in a long time, *but you're calling from a number they wouldn't recognize.* So you have to clarify who you are.

Remember, before they can ask any questions, you tag on **"how-you-doin'-today?"**

At this point, they may engage in conversation with you. They may say, "I'm doing fine how about you?" If so, I like to deepen the relationship with one of the following (depending on the time of year):

- **Just trying to stay warm, it's chilly out there isn't it?**
- **Just enjoying this weather, it's gorgeous out there isn't it?**
- **Just trying to stay dry, it's getting nasty out there isn't it?**
- **Just trying to stay cool, it's hot out there isn't it?**

Or they may not engage. They may just say "I'm fine," and not throw it back to you. If they try to brush you off like this, try to lighten the mood with a similar variation of the responses I listed above. Try something like:

- **Are you staying warm? It's chilly out there isn't it?**
- **Are you enjoying this weather? It's gorgeous out there isn't it?**
- **I hope you're staying dry; It's getting nasty out there isn't it?**
- **I hope you're staying cool, it's hot out there isn't it?**

Notice that these topics are all about weather, which seems odd for a sales call. This is a tip I got from Ricky Carruth, and it's dynamite. This makes you a real person. It localizes you to the same area they live in. You immediately have something in common even if it's just avoiding raindrops or sunbeams.

It's also more like a conversation you'd have with a friend. It tends to break the ice really quickly. You can also talk about a holiday (or even a local event) with one of the following:

- **Just looking forward to Christmas/New Year's/Valentines/The Game, ... How 'bout you?**
- **Just getting back from Thanksgiving/Labor Day/the 4th/etc. Was it a good break for you?**

Or if they don't engage:

- **I'm looking forward to Christmas/New Year's/Valentines/etc. Do you have big plans?**
- **How was your Thanksgiving/Labor Day/the 4th/etc.?**

The point here is to get them engaged in a bit of light conversation and put them at ease. You're not a telemarketer. You're not a person who wishes them harm. You're not calling to take advantage of them. You're a person, just like them. You want them to form an affinity with you.

It's very important to establish this little tidbit of conversation in your call script. It builds trust and likability in the prospect's mind. If they aren't connecting with you, it's because you aren't establishing this piece well enough in your call.

The next thing I usually move the conversation to is, "**Hey, I was just getting back in touch with you about our Facebook post... about the list of homes? Were you able to see the houses?**"

Then let the conversation flow. See what they're looking for. Ask if they were able to access the search portal. Not everyone who submits their information actually goes through to your site and checks it out. Make sure they got what they were looking for, initially.

When there's an uncomfortable pause at the end of the conversation, I say, "**Well, something I do for all my clients is a free Strategy Session to go over your goals for the house and help you put a solid plan in place to get there. Would it make sense to book an appointment like that for you?**"

"Would it make sense to..." is a wonderful closing question. I learned that phrase within the pages of James Muir's book "The Perfect Close." I highly recommend that book for an in depth discussion about phrasing key questions to move the sale to the next logical step.

Then give them an option for two days, "**Would Monday or Wednesday be better for you?**" Then give them an option for two time slots in whatever day they pick. "**Would 3:30 or 5 pm be better for you?**"

Boom! That's how you book an appointment from a Follow Up call. In fact, the entire point of your Follow Up Calls is to move a prospect toward a Strategy Session (appointment). That will allow you to dive deeper into their needs and find common solutions. That's the purpose of the **Conversion Cylinder**, which we'll cover in the next chapter.

Systems to Automate

CRMs

Immediately following our lead generation efforts, the next system that is an absolute necessity is a client relations manager or a CRM system. This system can receive your leads directly from Facebook, store all their contact information, send them an automatic email with information about the homes list they requested, as well as send automated follow up emails over the next several days introducing your home selling and buying systems. It can automatically email any buyer promotions that you run as well as helpful tips along the way.

The system I use is called **Follow Up Boss**. I love it for its ease of use and the ability to segment my leads into stages. I can track them easily from being an unconverted lead, to a hot prospect, to an appointment, to under contract, to being a past client. I can set up action plans for each of the stages, which means automated events (like emails, texts, or tasks) can be initiated as a lead moves from one stage to the next.

This system has allowed me to build a deep library of templated emails as well as text messages. Another great thing about the system is call tracking. Every phone call is recorded and timed. I can easily take notes as the conversation unfolds. At a glance, I can recall all the information a lead has given me and know exactly what I need to do to help them on the next communication.

Follow Up Boss also has a unique accountability tool that it calls the Leaderboard. This is a visual scoreboard that tracks your progress, and we use it within our team to motivate agents to outperform each other with a bit of fun competition. The Leaderboard assigns point values to all you Follow Up Activities.

For example, if you book an appointment, you automatically get 500 points. By the way, it ties into your Google Calendar which automatically confirms the appointment for you and the prospect through an automated email.

If you have a phone conversation with a lead lasting longer than two minutes, it gives you 100 points.

For a phone call attempt (unanswered), you'll recieve 10 points.

For a text message, 2 points.

For an email, 1 point.

You might notice that these points also follow the levels of effectiveness of communication which forces your mind to prioritize more productive activities. The way **Follow Up Boss (FUB)** designed this system is genius.

In a later chapter, Gauges, we'll see the importance of having this ability to track your activities, but for now just know that it's a great feature of the **FUB** CRM system. If you're using a different CRM you should try to track these metrics on your own.

Great thing about a CRM is that it can give you daily reminders of which leads to follow up with and what method of follow up to employ. This is all customized to your follow up plan. I would prioritize at least seven follow up attempts in the first three days of getting a lead.

In **FUB**, I've set these as tasks that must be completed for each lead. Those reminders keep me on task. It's highly engaging to click through that checklist every day.

If you'd like to use the same CRM my team and I use, just go to www.LoneRockHomeTeam.com/AgentResources. Depending on promotional timelines, you might be able to lock in a discount through my link on that page.

Appointment Booking Services

In addition to a great CRM, you might think about employing an appointment booking service. This is one way to outsource the task and free up more of your time for content creation or client work. While this is a great idea, I don't recommend that you completely depend on an outside service to close all your leads, but merely as a supplement to your own follow up attempts.

These services can take many forms, and I've tried many of them in the past. There are Facebook Messenger Chat Bots, automated text messaging platforms, and even Inside Sales Assistant companies for hire. All of them have the same basic goal, which is booking an appointment on your calendar via an app like Calendly or Appointlet.

I haven't had great results from fully automated systems, like drip text responders. And when I hired an overseas virtual assistant to make calls, the results were terrible in my case. My VA was leaving messages that didn't make any sense for the type of lead that they were supposed to be calling. It was a mess, and I had very upset potential clients calling me with very strong complaints. Not good.

Honestly, the best results I've gotten so far have come from a hybrid approach between automated emails from my CRM, personally making my initial calls/texts/videos to each lead (not outsourced) and having a semi-automated (but human monitored) campaign of text reach outs from a third party company. The company I use for Facebook ad management, Witly, also has a program to set appointments for you. They have set 6-8 appointments per 100 leads fairly consistently, which is a phenomenal addition to what my other systems are already doing.

I know that even if I'm not able to make all my calls as consistently as I aspire to, the bulk of my leads won't fall through the cracks. Again, go to www.LoneRockHomeTeam.com/AgentResources to see the special deal the Witly team has worked out for you there.

Assets

It's often helpful to have specific pieces of content to send to your leads to help with the conversion process. It may take months or years to develop all the Assets in this section, but they are well worth the effort. They will serve you well.

One of the best assets for you to develop is a **YouTube channel**. You can easily send a link via text or email to a YouTube video. Make sure to send a video that addresses a specific concern a lead might have, be it credit repair, different types of loan programs, or top tips to sell their house for more. Adding to your video library over time should be a to priority.

You can also have PDF assets. One of my favorites is a **Buyer's Guide**. This should include tips about the loan process, how an MLS search works, and negotiating tips.

My clients have also appreciated a **Moving Checklist** to help them stay organized during such a chaotic time.

My photographer created a **Photo Checklist** which is really handy guide to getting the house ready for Photo Day.

My **"Price Accelerator" video program** is now a great follow up asset when I have someone interested in selling their home. This is essentially a recorded listing presentation which answers all their questions on how to prepare their home to have the best presentation for the buyers. I've included all the different ways we will promote the home and explain how to be smart when pricing the home for maximum effect.

It's about a 20 minute conversation that I recorded one time, edited for a few hours with graphics, and now it can be used over and over again with every new client. It is a huge help for building authority and minimizing time at the listing appointment. Quite often, when I arrive at listing appointments, they don't have any questions about me as an agent, only about pricing strategy and then they're ready to sign the listing paperwork. It's now a foundational piece of my sales system that I'd never want to be without.

I also packaged the basic concept of that listing presentation into a physical **Magazine Style Brochure.** This is an asset that can be mailed to a prospect explaining what I do and why I'm different than other agents.

You should brainstorm all the different types of assets that can benefit your clients and systematically start to create these documents and videos as your career progresses. Try to create a new one every quarter. After a year or two you'll have a lot to offer. Your clients will see you as an expert authority on this subject matter. They will trust and respect you much faster with the help of these Assets.

Mass Follow Up

There are several types of Follow Up that can be sent to your entire database. Of course, many of your leads should be seeing your social media presence. This can almost be seen as another type of CRM.

Facebook follows up with my leads without any conscious effort on my part. This is why **video ads** are so powerful. As we saw above, it's one of the most effective forms of communication. For a few cents, we can put a message back in front of the people that are most likely to do business with us.

Within your **CRM** system you can easily communicate with your entire database of leads in one **email blast**. So, if you've created a particularly helpful YouTube video, why not share it with the database? If there's an interesting piece of news in your area that you want to make sure they all see, why not create an email about it?

However, the main email content you should prioritize is a **Weekly Email** to everyone in your database. I have mine set for Thursday morning. It's usually a weekly recap of any content that I've created on social media, including links to relevant local news articles, perhaps events.

My readers might be interested in blog articles on my website, so those are linked as well. I usually include local market graphics. I also link to different preset home list searches on my website (like from my Homes List ads), as well as direct links to helpful assets they can download from my website.

Every week, I craft a unique email from these elements and I blast it out to my entire database. This is something you should dedicate your yourself to being consistent with. Even if a lead never communicates with you directly, you can be in touch with them over the course of months or years until they are ready to make a move. At that point, you've been in their inbox every week and should be top of mind.

Make sure to schedule this **Weekly Email** into your calendar and make it a priority. It's a game changer for those who implement it.

Let's Rev it Up!!!

Next Steps:

1. Create your Follow-Up script.
2. Now practice it 50 times. Repetition is your friend.
3. Do you have a killer CRM in place? If not, research some CRMs now.
4. What assets have you built, or do you have access to? What are the next assets you'll commit to building over the next few quarters?
5. What types of mass Follow-Up can you build out? Get started!

<u>Cylinder #3</u>: Conversion

This is the stage where the business is won or lost. This is where true real estate professionals shine. Our lead generation efforts and our follow up conversations have all led up to this.

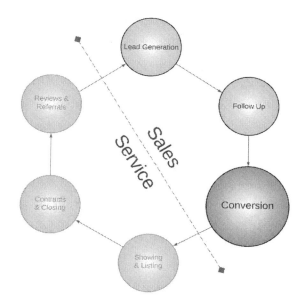

At this point, we will have a real conversation with our potential client to discover the problems they're trying to solve with a new house. We're going to craft solutions together to get them where they want to go.

To begin with, I'd like to say the traditional version of this process is called either a Buyer Consultation or a Listing Appointment. In my experience, no prospect wants to listen to a presentation from you. They don't want to sit there quietly, while you drone on and on about how great you are and how wonderful your services are.

I dislike having a prepared PowerPoint presentation or a flipbook for this process. In fact, I've changed the name of this stage for my clients to give it a completely different feel. **I simply call this a Strategy Session.**

So, whether I'm dealing with a buyer or a seller, I book this appointment as a Strategy Session. In any case, this is the cylinder that most requires you to develop deep sales skills. You'll need to learn how to establish rapport, ask the right questions, dig for deeper answers, and offer creative solutions to your prospect.

This will take time, attention and lots of practice. I've studied training material from some of the greatest sales coaches in the industry. I've consumed this content in many different forms: books, videos, seminars and hands-on in-person trainings. I've also spent hours role playing this both by myself and with peers and managers.

Across all the different sales training systems out there, I have found it helpful to boil them all down to a simple framework. I developed a process that's easy to remember and efficient to execute in the moment. It's helpful to know where the conversation is going so I can keep it on track and lead the conversation step by step. Allow me to introduce you to the **H-O-U-S-E-S Sales Formula.**

H – How've You Been?

O – Overview

U – Understand

S – Summarize

E – Expert Opinion

S – Solution

H – How've You Been?

Key Question: **"How've you been?"**

If you think about it, this question is rarely asked except by friends who are catching up after a long absence. When someone begins to answer this question, subconsciously, they are falling into a state of rapport with you. It's as if you've known each other for a while and your relationship has been positive. This question elicits a friendly mood, and it may result in a lifelong friendship by the end of this conversation.

So, take a few minutes to catch up with them about how their life is going right now. Feel free to discuss polite topics like the weather, local events, sports, and the like. If this meeting is taking place in their home, feel free to compliment the house during this portion of the conversation. Are there decor or interior design elements you really appreciate? Make sure to discuss those things.

Let the conversation go on for a few minutes. Try to find commonalities such as work experience, schools, and friends you might have in common. These bonds can go a long way in building a relationship. The classic **FORD** principle may be helpful as well: keep conversations safely centered around **F**amily, **O**ccupation, **R**ecreation and **D**reams. These topics will build trust and create more meaningful connections. Let this go on until these topics find a natural end.

When I sense a lull in the conversation, I move to the next phase and we get down to the real reason for the Strategy Session.

O – Overview

Key Question: "So tell me, **What's changed for you that's got you thinking about making a move?**"

This question is crafted strategically to draw out not only the motivation for the move, but also pinpoint the exact event that *caused them to decide* that they needed to move. Allow them to go into detail here. Dig deeper until you find the root cause.

A good follow up question to this is, **"Why now versus six months ago, or six months from now?"**

It's at this point that I usually break out a pen and paper and start taking notes. I want the conversation to flow, and to be based on what they want to accomplish, not on what I'm trying to sell them.

Another great set of follow up questions is, **"Why not just stay where you are? Is that an option?"** This reversal is a powerful way to help the client realize that NOW is the time, and there's a reason they need to take action. When they are asked to spell it all out for you, they often find a new level of motivation. Let them convince you that this move is necessary, and they'll be simultaneously convincing themselves.

As soon as I have a good **Overview**, I move on to the next step.

U – Understand

Key Questions:

- **"What's your biggest headache with your current living situation?"**
- **"What's the dream outcome? What are we trying to accomplish?"**
- **"Tell me more about that. Why is that important to you and your family?"**

This is the stage where we need to dig in deep, not just for ourselves, but also for the prospect to understand what they truly need and what they truly want. Many people have never thought deeply about their situation and they've never defined a clear outcome for themselves. This is one of the ways you can provide tremendous value as a sales professional. As an expert consultant, we need to help them understand the problems that are causing them pain right now and we need to help them develop a roadmap toward their dream outcome. (Their Dream House, most likely.)

Biggest Headache

- **"What's your biggest headache with your current living situation?"**

I love this question because it gets to the heart of all the negative things that people continue to live with. It's sometimes helpful to break this into another question:

"What are the top three things about this house that we want to avoid in your next house?"

Oftentimes, people will jump to what they do need, but briefly bring them back to the pain points and ask them to clarify what they don't want in their next place. It's also often helpful to go even deeper with clarifying questions like:

"Tell me more about that."

or

"What's the difficulty with that thing in particular?"

Once I've established a pretty clear view of negatives, I'll move on to the positive outlook.

What's the Dream

- **"What's the dream outcome? What are we trying to accomplish?"**

I like asking, **"What's the dream?"** because it fits with one of my core principles which is "I help people make their dreams come true."

If we can get someone close to living their dream life by the time we're done working together, I know I've done a great job and I'll probably have a client for life. I'll have a client who feels comfortable referring me to their friends & family, and they'll be bragging about their experience on social media. The review they leave will be phenomenal.

This question is also usually a breath of fresh air for the prospect. They've been dealing with a reality they aren't completely happy with. It allows them to think outside the box and open their mind to the possibilities in front of them.

It's at this stage that we can start to write down specifics about the home they want to buy. We need to get clear about location, size of the home, number of rooms, and purposes of those rooms. We need to understand not just what type of home they want to buy, but how they plan to live in that space.

This will help inform our home search and allow us to quickly comb through various properties to arrive at the winner. After this strategy session, we should be able to start the property search for them immediately based on the criteria that we define in this stage. Once we have a clear picture of what the client wants, both negative and positive, it's helpful to summarize their position and get their complete buy in.

S – Summarize

Key Question: **"So it sounds like we need to move you away from X, Y, and Z and move toward A, B and C. Is that right?"**

If they confirm "That's right," you know you're on the same page. It's crucial that we get their buy in here. Don't be surprised if they add some more detail at this stage, which is the point of a summary. It's our final point of clarification before moving on to solving their issues.

Don't underestimate the importance of this step. It may seem simple, and it is, but it is an anchor point in the process. It allows the client to declare "**This** is what I don't want in my life. And **That** is the goal I'm going to shoot for."

Once they confirm this for themselves, there's almost no stopping them from accomplishing it. You've walked them through a process that allowed them to declare publicly what they desire, what they're willing to pour their effort into. Now they just need some direction on how to make it all happen.

E – Expert Opinion

Key Question: **"May I make a recommendation?"**

This is the stage where you lay out the next action steps. You should display your market knowledge at this point to help them understand the ease or the difficulty with which they should be able to accomplish this goal. Discuss market conditions, absorption rate, available inventory, and what to expect when competing with other buyers and sellers.

You should lay out a clear path with all the extra action steps between where they are now and where they would like to be. You should make them aware of some of the dangers and pitfalls along the way. It's also helpful to share the stories of other clients you've had, who were in a similar situation and how they ultimately found success by working with you.

I'll get into more detail on some of these action steps later in the chapter, depending on whether we're trying to strategize for a buyer or a seller, or a client that will be both buying and selling. You may need to layout a transition plan from one house to the next. Just realize, this portion of the formula is intended for you to shine as the expert as you guide them into the next step.

S – Solution

Key Question: **"Would it makes sense to...?"**

You should present the very next action step on their journey immediately following the phrase, "Would it make sense to ..."

I learned this phrasing in the book *The Perfect Close* by James Muir. Again, I highly recommend this book to understand how to craft strong Closing questions for many different scenarios.

For buyers, it might be, **"Would it make sense to connect with a lender?"** For sellers, **"Would it make sense for us to decide on our opening weekend? What date would you like the home to hit the market?"**

This step is a closing question. This is us moving them from stasis, a static position, into action. This is getting them to take the first step toward working with us.

(Yes, this will ultimately lead to an agency agreement or a listing agreement. But at this point, I usually just present that as paperwork. "That's just the paperwork we need to get started." I downplay its importance a bit, as if it's just another thing that I'll handle for them to ultimately get them to their desired destination. When the time comes to sign it, of course I'll go into detail about the document and make sure they understand it all, and the rights and obligations it contains.)

Right now, what's important is that we decide on the next step, and we take it together. Then there may be another step immediately after that one, and we'll take that together too. And on and on, until they've achieved their desired outcome.

At the end of this **Solution** step, they should feel as if you've taken them on as a client, and you're eager to help. They should get the sense that, as long as they keep taking steps, you'll keep working hard for them.

Buyer's Strategy Session

The first part of our appointment with buyers will typically revolve around finding the criteria of the house that they want to buy. The next step is to determine their eligibility, seeing whether they're qualified to buy a home and at what price point. One of the biggest criteria for the houses we will look at is the price, so we need to know exactly what range of homes we should be looking at.

Unless they're planning to pay with cash, we will need to work with a lender to determine how much they can qualify for. And with a pre-approval letter from a lender, we can breeze right through the rest of the process all the way to the closing day.

If they're not already working with a lender, I like making some great recommendations for them. They'll need a loan officer at a dependable lending institution. A great loan officer will be able to help us decide which Loan Program and down payment level is right for the client.

When the lender is determining their eligibility, they look at many factors including job history, credit history, assets, etc. But there are 2 main criteria they look at the most: **Debt-to-Income Ratios** (DTI) and **Credit Score** (FICO Score).

Obviously, we can't pull their credit score, although we can certainly ask. Most people have a decent idea of what their score is. Ultimately, the loan officer will need to check it anyway. But a quick check on Credit Karma may be worthwhile at this stage.

If it seems their credit score is in a financeable range (~600+), we can often provide some value in helping them understand what payment level they will be able to qualify for.

To broach this subject, one of the most useful concepts I learned during my days as a new construction salesperson was the phrase "Buying Power."

Buying Power

Key Question: **"Has anyone cared enough to show you your buying power?"**

This is a quick and dirty estimation of their debt-to-income ratio, which will help you determine if they're even in the ballpark of being able to afford to make the payments on a home. This is especially helpful with first time homebuyers or people who aren't sure they can qualify for a loan.

"Has anybody cared enough to show you your Buying Power?"

Debt-to-Income Ratios

There are more regulations on mortgage lending than most other types of loans and credit, and one of those requirements is a hard line on the amount of someone's income that can be spent on a mortgage payment. In general, this is to protect the borrower from buying more home than they can afford.

And there are two factors in this calculation. There is a **Front End Ratio**, which is just the ratio of **Mortgage Payment to Income**. Then there is also a **Back End Ratio**, which includes **All Debt Payments**.

Front End Ratio

The Front End Ratio is **typically 29-33%** of their income (depending on the loan type.)

To Calculate this, add up all of their **Yearly Sources of Income**, including W2 work, 1099 work, Social Security received, Child Support, Alimony, etc. If they have a co-borrower, combine their numbers into one Total.

Then divide by 12 to get a **Monthly Income Total.**

Then multiply by **0.30**. This will give you a very general idea. (Again, different loan programs will have different **Front End Ratios**.)

Example:

$100,000 yr / 12 months = $8,333

Then $8,333 x 0.30 = $2,500

So, their monthly Mortgage shouldn't exceed $2,500 per month.

Next, we'll Calculate the **Back End Ratio (DTI).** Your maximum payment amount will be the lesser of the Front End and Back End numbers.

Back End Ratio (DTI)

The Back End Ratio is **typically 39-50%** of their income (depending on the loan type.)

To Calculate this, take the same **Monthly Income Total** you used for the Front End.

Then multiply by **0.41**. Again, this will give you a very general idea. (Of course, different loan programs will have different **ratios**.)

Then Subtract all your other **Monthly Debt Payments**.

Example:

$100,000 yr / 12 months = $8,333

Then $8,333 x 0.41 = $3,416.53

So, their total monthly Debt Payments shouldn't exceed about $3,415 per month.

Now Subtract all Debt Payments from $3,415 to determine how much room there is for the Mortgage.

$3,415 - $325 (Credit Card minimums) - $450 (Auto Loan) - $290 (1% of Student Loan) - $100 (Personal Loan) = $2,250

Notice this $2,250 is a lower number than the $2,500 Front End Ratio from above. So, their monthly Mortgage Payment shouldn't exceed $2,250 per month.

Lender Handoff

Once we've established that they are a fairly good candidate for a mortgage we should bring our loan officers into the picture.

Key Question: **"Would it make sense for me to connect you with my lending partner, Richard? He has some interesting programs going on right now that you may be able to qualify for."**

At this point, we can make a call to the lender together. Also text them the lender's contact information and the application form. You should already have a full contact card in your phone, completely filled out for each lender you recommend regularly. Make sure to have their cell and office phones, any relevant email addresses, and most importantly, the URL link to their loan application page stored in their contact card. I also like to save their photo in the contact card as well. It's easier for clients to make the association.

Seller's Strategy Session

When it comes to working with sellers, we have a lot of ground to cover, so much so that it's hard to fit it all into one Strategy Session. So, the first thing to keep in mind about listing properties is that you want to win before you arrive.

What that means is these people should have been getting videos, they should have been getting information, and communication from you long before we're sitting down together. They should have gotten the pre-listing video that we sent over. Make it clear that you need them to watch that before the meeting because it's going to answer most of the questions that they have. That way we can just talk about their house and their strategy when we get to the appointment.

Listing Packet

Also, it's important to have a **Listing Packet** in a nice folder for them. We will fill that with some of the assets we described earlier in **Cylinder #2: Follow Up.**

I include my **Magazine Style Brochure**, which goes through where buyers come from, the importance of visuals in our marketing, what our full marketing strategy is, a checklist of services. It's got our expectations and goals and the full 8 week marketing plan that I've laid out in here.

It's also nice to have a **Seller's Questionnaire** for them to fill out. We can use this to create a sheet for buyers to be able to see in the house. This would include things like,

- What made you buy this house?
- What are you going to miss most about this home?
- What are you going to miss most about the area or the neighborhood?
- What would you like to say to the people buying this home?

These are good questions to ask them that get them thinking about all the positives of the house. We can use these features in our marketing to the buyers to help boost how the buyers feel about the house, the neighborhood, the area, etc.

I also include some flyers, one about my **Social Media Marketing**, showing graphics of what our ads look like. This really sets us apart from other agents who just throw it in the MLS, put a sign in the yard and just hope and pray that it sells. I do proactive marketing to go out and find people for their house.

Of course, I also have my **Service Packages** and the corresponding commission levels. I always save this until the Listing Strategy Session, so this will be the first time the clients will see this information. It isn't posted publicly anywhere.

Then I also have a **Moving Checklist** as well as a **Photo Day Checklist**.

I may also include some extra **PostCard Samples** or other **Print Marketing** pieces for extra wow factor.

This **Listing Packet** is going to set you apart as a professional and it's going to shift how the homeowner thinks of you versus other agents who might show up with nothing.

CMA

Another thing to bring is a CMA, or a Comparative Market Analysis, to help the client understand how to price their house. We can do this CMA right in the MLS, so let's discuss some of the do's and don'ts of this process.

First of all, you want to find comparable properties that have sold no longer than **Six Months** ago, or the last time the market shifted. So if you're three months into a market shift, things from five or six months ago might not apply. But in general, in a normal market, six months is fine.

You want those properties to be located in the **Same Neighborhood** as the target property if possible. Within the "Map Search" function in the MLS, I'm always in favor of actually mapping out the exact boundaries of the neighborhood that the house is in, not just doing a diameter of half a mile or a mile away or something like that.

Don't cross **Major Roadways**. I've literally seen instances where houses on one side of the street are 250,000 and on the other side of the street they are 450,000. Those two valuations don't really affect each other, so they shouldn't be put in the same market evaluation.

Even within the same neighborhood, you want to segment properties by **Number of Stories**. Don't compare single stories to two stories. When compared to a single story that has the same square footage, a two story house has half the roof and half the slab, those are big costs in the construction. If it's a single story, make sure that in the search criteria, you're only looking for single stories.

Then you can also keep the **Sizing** of the houses within a fairly narrow range. The amount of square footage for those comparable houses should only be 15-20% above or 15-20% below the target house. So for example, if your house that you're evaluating is a 2,000 square foot house, maybe go down to 1600 square feet, and up to 2400 square feet. But do not compare a 2000 square foot house with a 1000 square foot house.

If you're in a neighborhood, that had homes built across different time periods, then you also need to segment by age of the homes. If the neighborhood wasn't all built at the same time, or the same couple of years span, try to segment the results into about a **10 Year Window** around the target house. If the house that you're evaluating was built in the 1990s, try not to compare it to a house built in the 1970s or to a house that was built five years ago. Keep those results within about a decade of each other.

Also, if it is an older neighborhood, take note of which comparable homes have been Remodeled and which are more original. Even though they were built around the same time, houses that have gone through **Remodeling** will sell for higher prices. Make sure you're comparing apples to apples.

Find as many of those comparables as possible with **Three being the Minimum.** The goal is to only use homes that are truly comparable to the subject.

We should also take into account the general pricing trends of the local market. What are the **ListPrice-to-SalePrice Ratios?** Are prices going up or down? Has the market shifted due to broader economic forces? What level are mortgage interest rates? What narrative are most buyers are hearing in the news? All of these factors should play into your pricing strategy.

Pricing & Commission

As for pricing strategies, at the end of the CMA, I like to figure out the **Average Price per Square Foot** of these comparable homes. Then I apply that number to the **Actual Square Footage** of our subject house. For instance, if the Average $/sqft of the comparables was $186 and my client's home was 1,613 sqft we would multiply those numbers together like this:

$186/sqft x 1,613 sqft= $300,018

Then I always like to put a 5-10% range around that. So in our example, I would go 5% above that price and 5% below that price. So, 5% below that price would be $285,000. Above it would be $315,000. That's about a $30,000 range.

This range depends on the sales prices of the comps too. If they are selling in a very narrowly defined range, if the price per square foot is very consistent, then you don't have to give as wide of a range.

However, I always present a range of value. The reason to give a range is because you want to express to the seller that you don't actually know what it will sell for. And neither does Zillow. And neither does any other agent that they talk to. There is no **"One Absolute Value!"** for any home.

Neither those other competing agents nor I are going to be the buyers. We won't be the ones writing the check.

I usually say something like, "The goal of a great agent is to help you present your property in a way that increases the **Buyers Perceived Value** of the property such that they give a higher price for it." Take note of the phrase, Buyer's Perceived Value. It's all about they perceive the property.

How we control perceived value is through the **Presentation** of the property. By Presentation, I mean cleanliness, curb appeal, staging, things like that. It's the way that property feels when you drive up to it and when you tour the property.

The next piece is **Promotion.** This is how the listing looks in the MLS. It's how the photographer crafts a compelling image of the property, how the video tour tells the story of that property. It's how we get it out on social media so that the most amount of people to see the property.

If we do those two things correctly, it will bring in the most amount of potential buyers which will result in the highest potential **Price.**

And that's why we give a range. Because the only thing most agents can really control is the Promotion. I've had good success in my career at also helping people with Presentation. It sets me apart from other agents because I let clients know I'm willing to hire a cleaner or a pressure washer or landscaper. I'm willing to do that as part of my listing package for them. I also have a listing package that is a full, whole-home staging and I will pay for that upfront.

However, it does increase the commission amount on the back end. As the commission package increases, so does the **Promotion and Presentation** of the property to the Buyers, thereby increasing the **Buyer's Percieved Value**. The benefit to the Seller is that with a higher commission Service Package, they can take comfort in listing at the higher end of the **Range of Value** supported by the comps, allowing them to **Net More Money** at the closing table.

That is how I'm able to consistently get beautiful listings that look amazing. Not only is it good for the homeowner, it's great for my business because now I have a gorgeous home to market that is clean and decluttered and picture perfect. I can go promote those pictures and those videos to tens of thousands of people.

I've literally had sellers pay me double the commission that another agent was charging. They chose me over the other agent because I provided so much upfront. They wanted those services and they saw the value in upping my commission to have it done.

They also got a phenomenal result in the marketplace that they probably wouldn't have gotten because the buyers flocked to the house. **In the end, they made more money with me than if they would have paid a lower commission.** I've seen this happen time and time again. My sellers consistently sell at 4-5% above the comps, even though the commission is only 1% above my competitors. Once it makes financial sense to them, I become the obvious choice.

It's important to be able to stand out in the Listing Strategy Session. It is all about what we do differently than what other agents do. It's your chance to make your service shine with so much professionalism that they want to do business with you versus all other options.

Again, one of the ways to stand out is having the total honesty to tell people, "I don't know what your house will sell for. But I know how to get it to sell for the most the market will bear!"

My side of the conversation often goes like this: "From the data, it looks like it should sell between a range of $285,000 and $315,000 based on what these other homes have sold for in the last couple of months. My recommendation is that if you don't plan to do all the preparation work that we've discussed, list it lower and it'll sell faster. But if you want to do some of this preparation work, or you're interested in some of the higher service packages that I offer, then I'm comfortable recommending going higher. I've seen that make such a difference for the buyers."

"Just those couple of percentage points in commission and some extra elbow grease can literally make $20,000 difference in your sale price. I know that sounds crazy, but it's true. And you can see it in the CMA. Sometimes even very similar homes can sell for $15,000-$25,000 difference."

You may have noticed this in a CMA before and you think "why is that?" Well, it's because those three properties had three different buyers. And those three different buyers believed that the houses were worth what they gave for them at the time. So the goal is to find the buyer who will give you the most. Again, it comes back to **the Buyer's Perceived Value** of the property.

Explain all this to your Seller, and then let them decide on the price after they looked through al the data.

Key Question: **"Given all we've discussed, what Listing Price do you think <u>would make sense</u> for the current market?"**

Ultimately, it's their house, it's their money, and it's their decision. I rarely fight a seller over their pricing. I just want them to have all the data and make an informed choice. The only caveat to that is if I'm spending thousands of dollars in the Preparation/Presentation on a high-end service package, they'd better be realistic in their Pricing. The top end of the range I give them is the highest I'd like them to go. I'm not interested in pricing it unrealistically high and just hoping it sells. I need assurance that it will close, and a realistic price is the most surefire way to get it done.

Timing

As for timing, I would always recommend trying to get at least two weeks to prepare the listing before they want it to go live in the MLS.

Key Question: **"Ideally, when would it make sense for the property to go live on the market? What fits best for you?"**

I think most people should probably be in touch with their agent and have the plan in place about a month out. It normally takes about two weeks for most people to **De-clutter, De-personalize, and Deep Clean.** They'll need to take some things to storage, drop off extra clothes at Goodwill, pull weeds from the flower bed, simplify this room, carpet clean that room, etc. We may have to schedule a stager, and we may have to schedule other services to help get it ready as well.

After that, we would ideally like about two weeks to get the marketing prepped for them. We have to schedule a photographer, And then we'll have to get our marketing package ready. Photos and videos need to be shot. Both of those things need to be edited, then delivered to us, then we have to build social media ads, and we we may also do a postcard announcement to their nearest 200 neighbors.

So, Presentation usually takes about 2 weeks, and Promotion usually takes about 2 weeks as well. This is why I try to meet with potential sellers as early as possible, even if they aren't planning to move for several months. It gives everyone plenty of time to schedule all the important pieces.

Ending the Strategy Session

Whether we're meeting with a Buyer or a Seller, the client should now have a clear idea of what their next steps are. They should also know all the next steps you'll be taking on their behalf.

For Buyers, we should be able to start a property search for them and we should be on the path toward acquiring their

PreApproval Letter from the lender (or Proof of Funds if they're a cash buyer.) You may even want to schedule your first home tour at this point, just to block out the time for them in your calendar. Then, if they aren't finding anything they want to see in your MLS auto-property searches, you can reschedule. The point is to move the process as far along as they're comfortable with, and keep asking them **"would it make sense"** to take the next step.

For Sellers, ideally we will leave the Strategy Session with a signed **Listing Agreement**, detailing the date it will be listed and the Listing Price they'll be asking the market to deliver. They should have also chosen a Service Package and corresponding commission amount as well. Once we've worked out all the details in conversation, I usually just pull out the Listing Agreement and start filling it out with all the relevant information.

I ask their preferences on the remaining items like offering home warranties, any items they do or don't want to sell with the house, and any special requirements. We discuss all the main sections of the Listing Agreement, and I give a brief synopsis of each. Even if they mention they don't want to sign the contract at this time, I say "That's perfectly fine. I'll still fill it out with all the information you've decided on so far, so I don't forget. When you're ready, I'll use this to send you an E-Sign session, and then we'll be able to get started."

The end of any Strategy Session should help them feel more confident in their decision to move forward. They should know their next steps, and you should have invited them to take as many action steps as possible. I've had Buyers leave a Strategy Session prequalified with the lender, showings scheduled for the next day, and they closed on their new home 21 days later.

126

Go as fast as they're comfortable going. It's not your job to be the Brake! But you can't push the accelerator for them either.

Let's Rev it Up!!!

Next Steps:

1. Learn and Master the H-O-U-S-E-S sales strategy. Practice it 50 times.
2. Learn and master the "Buying Power" formula.
3. Do you have a Listing Packet?
4. What about a Listing Video? Make plans for it.
5. How's your CMA process? Does it need a revamp?
6. Get comfortable asking "Would it make sense to...?"

Part 3: The Service Engine

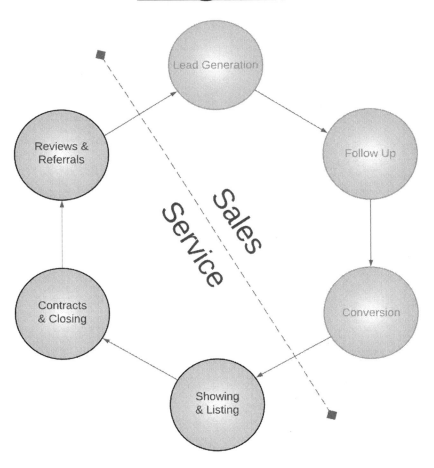

Cylinder #4: Service- Showing and Listing

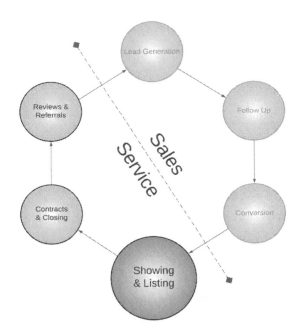

This is where the rubber meets the road. This is where our superior service separates us from the competition.

The biggest businesses with the biggest brands in the world usually get that way by having the best product or service in their sector. What they provide the customer is so good that the customer can't help but tell their friends and family about it. Oftentimes, these products and services go viral and spread throughout the community in a way that makes the business a dominant player in their space.

We want our service to be so good that clients can't help but tell everyone they know about us. When they hear somebody at their workplace talking about selling their house and making a move, we want them to say, "You gotta talk to my guy!" and then immediately give them our number. Let's explore how we can build a system that delivers unmatched results for our clients.

Relationships with Vendors

The first concept to realize is that you are only as strong as your team. You may think that as an individual agent, you don't have a team. You really do. All of the other service providers and professionals that you surround yourself with determine the outcome that your clients will experience. We've talked about some of our key players so far, but here's a more thorough list:

Lenders

This may be your most important ally in the fight to get your clients into their dream home. I recommend having great relationships with the mortgage officers in your area, having at least three go-to winners that you would trust with your own mortgage.

I try to have a mix of lenders that have good solutions for different problems. I have one from our most popular **local bank**. I have another one that's an **independent mortgage broker**. This allows him to shop for different programs and craft creative solutions to our clients situation. I have other great relationships at the **lender most of the new construction home builders** use.

It's probably also a good idea to expand your sphere to include **commercial lenders, land lenders,** and maybe even **farm or specialty** types of lending.

Title

You should also have a couple of great title companies you recommend your clients work with. I like to choose companies that have a great track record of closing on time and doing thorough research. They should be well known names in the local marketplace. Since my clients will be going to their offices to sign documents on closing day, I like for their offices to feel upscale, clean, and modern. It makes the clients' experience a high-end ordeal, even on an average home. All of these things ultimately affect how my clients feel about working with me as well.

Inspectors

It's important to have a basket of inspectors available for your clients. I like to have a mix of inspectors that have a lot of experience in the field. They should work with good technology both to inspect the home systems but also to deliver the report in a timely manner. It may also be helpful to have a budget friendly inspector on your list.

Specialty Diligence Contractors

Depending on your area, you may need to have certain specialty inspectors or contractors available to review properties. These might include perc testers, septic system designers, radon testers, or mold and restoration specialists. Just look at the issues that can arise in your area. Make sure you have connections with professionals that can solve these problems before you're even under contract. Again, this is the value of thinking **Three Steps Ahead.** You should have solutions to problems before your client is even aware there is a problem. Having the right connections allows you to do so.

Property Prep Specialists

As part of my listing packages, I often include extra services like pressure washing, maid service or landscaping. All of these specialists have helped my career grow by allowing me to offer something that my competition doesn't. Your list of property prep specialists could also include movers, storage facilities, carpet cleaners, window washers, and the like.

Stagers

A great stager is like an interior designer, professional organizer, and expert marketer all rolled into one. They understand how to organize the space in a way that appeals to the mass market, thereby increasing the Buyer's Percieved Value. They may bring in furniture, artwork, and décor to increase the appeal of the home. I always offer my listing clients the option of using my preferred stager, especially if the home they are selling will be vacant during our listing period. Having an empty space makes the stager's job much easier because they can control the entire aesthetic of each room without having to figure out what to do with the owners' stuff. My favorite stagers also have connections with cleaners and handymen who can help prepare the property and handle any issues that may arise.

A professional stager uses the space in a way that taps into human psychology to make it more appealing. For instance, they may employ the strategic use of mirrors to allow the buyers to literally "see themselves" in the space. This goes beyond the advice of "depersonalizing" by removing the seller's family photos, and it actively places the buyers in the home, "personalizing" it to them instead. Stagers are full of interesting in-person marketing tricks like this.

When using a stager, not only will the buyers feel like they've stepped into an HGTV magazine during a showing, but the photos and videos of the space will literally "Pop" as well. Buyers will show up excited to see the home because they saw beautiful images of it online. They're already anticipating that they'll fall in love with it.

I've seen this effect raise sale prices by 4-5% over what the neighborhood averages would have originally indicated. A great stager is an invaluable member of your team as they'll bring tremendous results for your clients.

Photo/Video

These professionals are responsible for much of the professional presentation of your brand. In addition to getting magazine quality photos of your listings, they can also be instrumental in helping you create marketing content for yourself, be it headshots, property walkthrough videos, or helpful tips videos.

Since I started my career shooting listing photos and videos, I'm particularly picky about who I hire to do those tasks. One pro tip when evaluating a photographer's portfolio: check the verticals. Look at the corners of the rooms in all of their pictures and make sure that they're perfectly straight and perpendicular. Amateurs will often hold their camera at an awkward angle making the room look top heavy or bottom heavy and distorting the space. This is an easy way to separate the true professionals from the rest.

Then I also look at their use of lighting. Is the room evenly lit? Or are there dark corners, weird shadows and other distractions from what should be a beautiful presentation?

As for video, do they offer aerial drone service or just a standard walkthrough video. The drone can often add a wow factor you can't accomplish any other way. However, they'll need proper licensing with the FAA to operate in most jurisdictions.

Also, do they only do property video or can they capture audio too? Surprisingly, it throws some videographers for a loop when you ask to be included in the video. This is because they're used to getting the clips without sound and then overlaying music on top. They might not have a professional microphone to be able to record your voice.

If you're looking for a great photographer/videographer in your area, I recommend doing several searches on Instagram using your location as a search criteria. Because Insta started out as a photo platform, it still has a lot of engagement from photographers. I have found several of my favorite photo professionals on that platform.

Handyman

It's important to have a good handyman not only to help with property preparation, but also to quote repairs for your buyers during their inspection period. It's often helpful to understand what a specific repair might cost before jumping into negotiations with the seller. This type of connection could also include painters, roofers, flooring specialists, and any other construction trade that would work on the house.

Investors

Sometimes you'll run across an opportunity that might be good for an investor, be it a house flipper or someone looking to buy and hold real estate long term. Sometimes these individuals can provide creative solutions for your clients that you might not have thought of.

If someone is trying to list a house that needs a lot of work and it's apparent that they won't be able to get top dollar, perhaps an investor that offered them a fair price for it

would be a good solution. Then they'll do the renovations necessary, sell it at market value, and make a profit for themselves.

They can also provide creative funding solutions such as owner financing for your buyers, or they can take over payments for a homeowner who's behind with their bank. I recommend checking out biggerpockets.com and joining their forum to meet local investors in your area. That website is also tremendously helpful for understanding creative deal structures and all the ways that people make money as real estate investors. Throughout your career, you should study these techniques not just to understand them for your clients, but eventually to use them yourself and grow your own wealth through an asset class you know very well.

Constant Communication

One of the biggest ways clients judge an agent is by how often and how well they communicate. I let my clients know that I will be in touch with them at least once every week during the course of us working together. Even a quick text every time you have a new piece of information will make a huge difference by the time you close the transaction.

I recommend you have **Template Emails and Template Text** messages saved in your CRM for every major step along the client's journey from initially reaching out about their Homes List request, all the way through asking for reviews after the closing, and every single step along the way. Your library of Templates should grow throughout your career.

You should also brainstorm ways of communicating with your clients in unexpected ways. A Video Text instead of a voicemail can brighten someone's day. Weekly photos of a home under construction can really illuminate the process for a client. Plus, you can load all of those photos into a photo book as a closing gift. These are very unexpected and very appreciated. It's one reason I love selling new construction homes.

As simple as it sounds, continuing this constant communication all throughout the process really does make us stand out as professionals.

Providing educational updates and materials is another way to over communicate for your clients. The content you produce across all your social channels is just another layer of communication for those clients. You can bring tremendous value to your clients and community through this content creation.

Listing 3 P's

We touched on these during our Conversion chapter, but it's worth fleshing out the philosophy behind how **Pricing, Presentation, and Promotion** all influence the Buyer's Perceived Value. If you just focus on these 3 factors with your sellers, you'll be far ahead of most agents.

Traditionally, there were only a few things you could do to sell a house. Most agents relied on the **Old 3 P's**: **Put** a sign in the yard, **Put** it in the MLS, and **Pray** it sold.

But that simplistic method of selling could leave your home unsold in today's digital age. You see, we can do so much more now. And buyers expect much more. Also, we've never had more data at our fingertips to help make good decisions. It's important to embrace the new technology we have at our disposal, and to exceed the buyers' expectations.

When it comes to selling a home, most sellers want two things: a **Great Price** that protects their equity and a **Fast Closing** so they can move on with their lives. In order to ensure these two goals, we need to consider a few core principles I like to call **"The NEW Three P's of Home Sales:"** Price, Presentation, and Promotion.

(Just to give credit where it's due, I learned this 3 P's concept from Garry Creath & Chris Scott at *The Paperless Agent* and *Creath Partners Real Estate* in Austin, TX. It has been a huge advantage for my clients.)

Price

The first and most important piece of the sales puzzle is **Pricing it Right**. Buyers search for homes by price first, and all other criteria second. Pricing is critical, so working with a professional who is knowledgeable about current market trends is absolutely vital.

The strategy of **"Testing the Market"** by pricing high and then coming down later may actually be dangerous for your Seller's equity, not to mention it hurts your ability to close quickly. Most buyers won't even look at a property they feel is overpriced. Remember, they have access to similar data on what other homes have sold for nearby. Also, when you do start dropping the price, buyers see a property dropping in price week after week, and they begin to think you'll keep dropping, even past market value. This strategy often results in low offers, and limited ability to negotiate a higher marketable price.

Based on our CMA research, let's say the homes that sell, usually sell for **99-97%** of the listing price. However, this doesn't mean we can just list it at any price we want and expect to receive 97% of that price. Notice the most important part of that statistic, **"homes that sell..."** Not every home will sell, (even in a hot market) and overpricing is one of the main reasons.

If we deconstruct that statistic, we can determine at what price we should list your house. Let's change it to this: **Homes that sell, LIST for only 1-3% above MARKET PRICE.** (This List-to-Sell Price Ratio should be researched in every CMA.) Listing in this range will dramatically improve your chances of selling quickly while saving as much Seller equity as possible. More than that, and you'll risk lower interest, fewer showings, and lower offers.

The key is finding the market price, based on recent sales. Our CMA process (discussed in Cylinder #3: Conversion) will help us be in tune with the current market prices and trends.

Presentation

Homes for sale must **show well** to potential buyers and must be **easy to show** in order to get the most buyer attention. This is why I partner with local professional home stagers to get my clients' homes showcase ready.

Staging your home for sale helps ensure your equity and supports your pricing. An immaculate dwelling is hard for buyers to throw lowball offers at. Presentation supports the Price, so if you're going to price your listing at the top of the market, it better show like the Top-of -Market homes.

Everything from de-cluttering, de-personalizing, organizing, and cleaning all the way to repainting, repairing, and renting furniture & decorations can be considered "**Staging**." Work with your homeowner and stager to identify the best strategy for the home to make sure it shows the best for the budget you have.

Put together a showing schedule for other agents to be able to show the house. This should coordinate with an automated showing service, such as ShowingTime, which allows agents to book appointments directly from an app. It's important that the home stay in showcase ready condition for each of those showings.

Promotion

When the home goes out across the **MLS, Trulia, Zillow, Realtor.com**, and more, it needs to be represented in the best possible light.

There's no second chance at a first impression. The purpose of great photography and video is to get buyers' attention and make them want to see the house in person. All my listings get **Magazine Quality Photos** as well as a **Full HD Video**.

Acceptable photography isn't a quick walk around with an iPhone. Your photographer should bring in top of the line professional cameras and multiple lighting options. In fact, plan to have a full "Picture Day" to capture all the still photos and video content. The home will be shot from multiple angles and we will feature all the amenities that will make buyers fall in love with the house.

Don't go cheap here. It pays to hire a great photo/video professional. Yes, they cost more, but the images and videos they create are a representation of your brand. Always protect your brand's image through high quality visuals.

Cheesy slideshows of bad pictures set to music are a thing of the past. Buyers are now utilizing real video to get a feel for the house, and it often serves to make them feel that the in-person visit is like a second showing, increasing their connection to the space. Every home should get its own video on YouTube, the world's 2nd largest search engine, second only to its parent company, Google, which ranks YouTube content very highly.

Your home listing should also be distributed across the various **Social Media** channels to draw the most attention from the marketplace. But keep in mind, many of these channels really are "Pay-to-Play" and you should have a marketing budget set aside to put your listing in front of the masses through paid ads on these platforms. For example, in my business, it's not uncommon for me to promote a property and generate 40,000 to 50,000 impressions. That means tens of thousands of people saw the ad for that property. (Adding 1,000-2,000 Thruplays to our Alpha List!) And as we all know, more Ad Reach means more potential offers on the house as well as more potential clients for us.

Again, all this extra effort results in a protection of equity and a speedy sale. Each home should get the **Premium Treatment** so that you can **sell it for a premium** on the open market.

Listing Service Packages

As I mentioned earlier, I offer my listing clients multiple options. I don't just have one commission when they ask, "What's your commission?" I say, "Well it depends on what you want. What are you looking to accomplish?" That leads to a deeper discussion of what they actually expect in an agent.

This also allows me to advertise "Flexible commission rates, Only pay for what you need." However, this doesn't mean I'm a "discount agent." I don't offer deeply discounted services. However, my bottom package is about 10% off of what most clients from my area are expecting to hear. If there ever is a commission objection, I can point to that and say, "Well, my service is already discounted by 10% if you want my standard commission package." Even if I do eventually need to negotiate the commission with a stubborn seller, I never lower by a full percentage point. A few tenths of a percent should be enough to haggle over.

I have **Standard, Enhanced, and Premium Package** options. The fact that they get to choose between three different options solves most "commission slashing" objections outright. The **Standard** commission package includes a full service listing like they would expect from any competing agent. The **Enhanced** package includes help with property presentation. It has a budget of half a percentage point (0.5%)vthat will go toward that presentation. This could include services like pressure washing, maid service, carpet cleaning, landscaping, etc. I pay for that outright before listing and only get paid upon closing. It also includes a video walkthrough and social media promotion. The **Premium** package includes everything in the Enhanced package but I'm also paying for a stager upfront, but I charge a full percentage point more at closing.

These commission structures and service packages have served my clients well, consistently delivering great results. In fact, the clients who choose the Premium package are almost always happier with their results; they net more money even after the additional commission expense. Plus, I clearly standout from my competition, a difficult task in an industry as competitive as ours.

Special Buyer Programs

For buyers, not only do we work with lenders that might have special mortgage programs, but I frequently offer specialized services for my buyers as well. One of those would be the Dream Home Finder program where I will prospect directly for homes that fit their criteria, even if those homes aren't currently listed for sale. So for instance, they can pick a neighborhood, pick a size of home, and a likely price point. Then I will set about finding properties that match that description and reach out to the homeowners directly, both by mail and by phone if necessary.

Another offer I've made is that if someone is selling a home with me and then turning around and buying their next home through me I will cover the cost of a professional moving service. This is another incentive to work with me versus all other agents. And it's a creative, out of the box program that I haven't heard many other agents contemplate.

Ultimately, your buyers may be best served simply by your market and product knowledge along with your deal making experience. For instance, if you understand how homes are constructed from the ground up and you know all the parts and pieces of the home, you can speak with authority when issues come up in inspections. Also, when your clients have a home under construction, this knowledge is invaluable and is a key part of the service that you provide. I recommend attending all inspections and learning all you can from your inspectors.

Let's Rev it Up!!!

Next Steps:

1. Put together your list of Vendor Partners
2. Do you have template emails and texts loaded into your CRM, ready to go? If not, brainstorm the topics and conversational threads you'd like to automate.
3. Do you remember the 3 P's? Get comfortable enough with them that you can freely discuss them in conversation.
4. Do you have different listing service levels? Make a list of services you would like to include.
5. Any special buyer promotions you'd like to implement? Make a list.

Cylinder #5: Contracts and Closing

"We're under contract!" is my second favorite thing to say as a real estate agent, right behind **"It's closing day!"**

Putting a client under contract often brings feelings of elation and relief. But don't get too comfortable because we have a lot of work to do before the closing day can come.

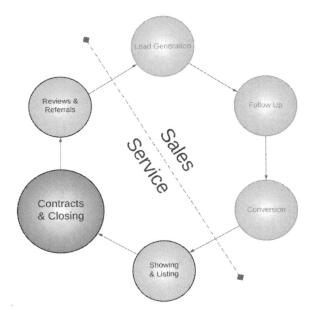

This is the time you'll be working hand in hand with your preferred vendors and you'll be in the most communication with the client. This is really the time period that can make or break the relationship with the client. It determines whether you'll be working with them for years to come, or if they'll break off the relationship prematurely. Plenty of deals fall out of contract. But my goal with this chapter is to minimize that number as much as possible for you.

Write 20 Contracts

The first key is to actually write a good contract and to understand everything in that contract like the back of your hand.

When I first joined the builder, management was upset with the lack of attention to detail that many of the sales team were putting into their contracts. Initials were missed on various pages. Certain seller incentives didn't make it in the contract. Sometimes, not all of the supporting documentation would be submitted. There were multiple problems, but out of frustration, my manager told me that as a new trainee, I'd be required to write 20 practice contracts before I would be allowed to start selling for real.

So, two days later I showed up with almost a full ream of paper and slammed down the 400 pages on his desk. Triumphantly, I said, "There you go!"

He looked at me in awe and said, "What's this?"

"Those are the 20 contracts you told me I had to write."

He laughed it off a little bit and said, "I didn't think you'd actually do it!"

But there inside that stack of pages laid countless lessons that I had taken to heart while I was reading through each line of the contract and working out what everything meant.

I recommend you do the same. While you might not print them all out and slam them on a brokers desk, you should at least read through the contract dozens of times to the point that you can explain every section, paragraph and line to a client. I make this recommendation because your clients will ask you what a random phrase means or how this clause applies to that one.

You should have a good professional answer, ready to go. This will also help you write your contracts more quickly and easily. When an offer needs to be submitted and you're under the gun, you can quickly move through the process and get your forms submitted.

This also means you need to be proficient with your electronic signature software. You should know how to add the contacts, create a new transaction, add the documents, and move to e-signing with ease. This can only come through practice and repetition. It becomes solidified in your mind by actually going through the motions of doing a contract and sending it to your own email address. Twenty or more practice contracts will give you the repetitions necessary to become proficient.

Stay Educated

Every state in the US requires agents to have continuing education courses and I recommend that you don't blow them off. Take these training sessions seriously. Get as much information as you can from your instructors.

While the online classes are easy and quick to crank out in a pinch, I really prefer to be in a classroom with other students and a seasoned instructor that I trust. It allows me to ask better questions. It allows me to get answers that might not be in the course material.

Also, most real estate commissions change contracts and forms on a yearly basis. Make sure you're up to date on what those changes mean for you and your clients.

I went to check a box that I had been checking for years on contracts. It had always said the title fees were to be split evenly among the seller and the buyer. However, because it was a new form from the latest yearly update, that box now obligated my seller clients to pay the full amount if the buyers didn't close at the same title company. Sure enough, we got down to closing and my clients owed an extra $500. They weren't happy about it. Needless to say, I decided it was going to come out of my paycheck. My error; my penalty. So make sure you know all the changes that happen and ask your broker to go over them in detail at the beginning of every year.

Hire a TC Early

The last recommendation that I'll make here is that you hire a **Transaction Coordinator** early in your career. Not only will a great transaction coordinator save you time, but they might catch details that you had missed.

When I hired my first transaction coordinator, it changed my life forever. I instantly knew I would never go without one. The service they provide is well worth the money if they are a detailed and organized person, especially if that's not your personality type.

You might be thinking, "I'm just starting out. I can't afford to pay someone." Usually, you can hire a transaction coordinator by the individual transaction. You don't have to put someone on salary or commit to a certain number of months of paychecks. They usually charge a few hundred dollars, and only after the closing occurs, so they get paid after you get your commission.

A TC can save you so much time. That time can then go into your follow up efforts and lead generation marketing, thereby growing your business by leaps and bounds. I recommend you make this key hire as soon as you're comfortable within your career.

Let's Rev it Up!!!

Next Steps:

1. Write 20 contracts. Really. Schedule a day to do that.
2. Make a list of skills you'd like to learn and develop a plan to conquer them.
3. Do you have a Transaction Coordinator? If not, research a few in your area and make appointments to get to know them.

Cylinder #6: Reviews and Referrals

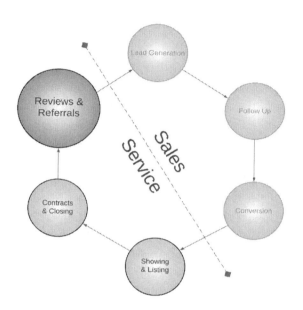

The most neglected of all 6 cylinders is probably number Six, dealing with **Reviews and Referrals**. So many agents go into closing, collect a commission check, cash it and never talk to those people again. This is a travesty, and it shows a serious lack of professionalism within our industry.

One of my mottos is "Once a client, always a client." I never want to stop providing real estate services to the clients that I've helped in the past. I don't want to forget them, and I definitely don't want them to forget about me.

I want the relationship to last a lifetime if possible. If you think about how many times people buy and sell real estate throughout their lives, the value of a single client could be Tens if not Hundreds of Thousands of dollars over the course of your career. Don't throw that away to go chase a new lead for every deal. If done correctly, this cylinder can allow exponential growth to take off in your business.

If you have clients that had a great experience, chances are high that they are willing to leave glowing reviews and send your name out as a referral to all their friends and family. You now took the cost of lead generation for one client and you've multiplied the return across multiple transactions, both now and into the future. You didn't have to pay extra for the leads which led to those closings.

This is why on our 6 Cylinder diagram, the arrow moves from Reviews & Referrals back to Lead Generation. Those past clients can now fuel the next generation of growth in your business and become lead generators themselves.

Review Process – Pre & Post Closing

One of the most important agreements I make early on with my clients is that they will leave a review at the end of the process. I often mention this even in the Strategy Session, well before we've listed a house or opened a lockbox. I tell them:

"If at any point in the process of working with me, you feel that I'm not living up to a level of service that you would be thrilled to give me a glowing five-star review, I want you to tell me immediately! Hold me accountable to exceeding your wildest expectations. That's the level of service that I strive to provide. And all I ask in return is that you leave that type of review at the end of the process. Fair enough?"

Then once we've got it under contract, I may bring it up again and ask, "How's my review looking?"

Of course, upon closing day, I'll send a final email with all their files from the transaction. I thank them for their business and asked for the review. I leave a link to all the sites that I would appreciate a review on, but I reiterate that my Google reviews are my main focus.

A few days after closing, if they haven't done the review, I might send a text that says,

> "Hey, I know you've probably been busy moving. I just wanted to make sure the Google review link didn't get lost in your inbox. So here it is again. Hope you're doing well. Let me know if there's anything else I can help with."

Even if it takes a few more reminders. It's well worth the effort to get the review from them. The more reviews you have, and the more stars in those reviews, the higher you will rank in Google's search results.

If you have clients that do a lot of posting on social media and are comfortable on camera, you might ask for a video review. This can be incredibly helpful in your advertising efforts. Imagine sending out several video reviews to your Alpha and Omega lists on Facebook. It can have a huge impact on how they perceive your service.

In any case, even without the video, you should be posting testimonials and reviews. Create images of the reviews and post them on your social media. Then promote those back to your audiences.

I've had many clients who've chosen me based purely on the reviews they found online. Don't overlook the crucial importance of reviews.

Referrals – Staying in Touch

To elicit more referrals, the best bet is simply keeping in touch with those clients for the long haul. There are many agents who've made a career out of working with only their past clients and referrals. They've built their business up to the point that they can completely stop advertising outside of their sphere of influence.

That's a powerful place to be, especially if you simply want to maintain a certain level of production year over year. At that point, your client base doesn't necessarily need to grow by leaps and bounds. However, if you do continue growing and building your audience, generating more leads, those past clients remain a stable base and allow your business to go parabolic.

Social Groups

One of the easiest ways to keep in touch is to continue using social media. Of course, your past clients will still be on your weekly email list. They'll also continue to see ads on their social media platforms as you roll out new content. But I have found it helpful to create a VIP group only for my clients. It's called **"Colley's NWA VIPs (Friends and Family)."**

Within that group, I'll post our Hometown Highlights videos. I post quizzes. I post funny pictures and ask people to caption them. My wife and I post interesting home interior trends, and also bad listing photos that people can laugh at. We post behind the scenes content and sometimes even family content.

One of the most fun things we've tried is to run a monthly contest with a prize. The prize is usually a ticket to some local event that people are excited about, or a gift card to a local small business or restaurant. The contest can be as simple as a photo titled, "How many candy corn are in this jar?" The closest guess wins.

This group fuels engagement both with myself and my family, but also the local community. It's not purely real estate focused, but there are subtle reminders that I'm their Realtor® of choice. It's a really fun way of keeping in touch, and all the group members really seem to enjoy it.

If you'd like to see the platform we use for fun, creative content, check out Social Orchard. If you go to the resources page on my website, www.LoneRockHomeTeam.com/AgentResources , you can find Social Orchard there.

Magazines

Another way to keep in touch that adds a very professional touch is to give to your past clients a magazine subscription. My favorite one comes from Reminder Media, and it's called American Lifestyle. It allows you to brand the front cover with your headshot and logo. You can edit the "letter from the editor" at the beginning of the magazine as well as the back inside and outside covers. It's high gloss and printed on high quality paper.

It makes me stand out as a professional. My clients appreciate the articles which are focused on home design trends, travel, and food recipes. Again, I've worked out a discount with Reminder Media for 66% off their onboarding fees. You can check it out at www.LoneRockHomeTeam.com/AgentResources .

Reminder Media also offers digital posting solutions as well as postcard campaigns. They have many different solutions for engaging content. You can also check out the Reminder Media "Stay Paid" podcast. They're constantly putting out great information.

Gifts

I always try to have a gift for my clients at the closing table. I just think it's a nice gesture and it solidifies the celebration of the moment. Some of the favorite gifts that we've given have been Boca Terry bathrobes. These elegant robes are used in some of the finest hotels and they really have a luxury feel. You can even get the clients' initials monogrammed onto the robe.

Of course, a well thought out gift basket is always nice as well. We typically pack these with all the essentials someone might need when moving into a new space. We include cleaning sprays, wipe, brushes, rubber gloves, as well as snacks and a few rolls of toilet paper (carefully wrapped in gift tissue paper that matches our brand colors.) Then we wrap it all with a cellophane sheet and top it with a bow. At the closing table the gift is delivered with a handwritten note to convey my appreciation.

Even after closing, the gifts can keep coming. We like to do a quarterly gift to our top 100 clients (the best referrers). We've sent them wildflower seeds at Spring time, random Starbucks gift cards for $5, and we even delivered these cookies during the holidays:

We hand delivered them to the door. It was a great way to catch up with some of the clients - the ones that were home anyway. These were hand decorated cookies from a local bakery with festive icing art for Halloween, Thanksgiving, and Christmas all in the same box. Hence the Happy "All"-idays!

The gift doesn't have to be extravagant or expensive. Just something that lets them know you were thinking of them. It's probably worth brainstorming several dozen ideas. You might try Googling "real estate pop -by gifts" a la *Work By Referral* by Brian Buffini. Also, read *Gift-ology* by John Ruhlin for creative gifting ideas.

Events

Another angle I'm anxious to get into is Client Appreciation Events. Many agents and teams around the country host an event once a year for their clients, usually in conjunction with fundraising for a local charity or cause that people can get behind. I've heard of movie nights at the park, renting out an entire bowling alley, or having a huge Christmas party or New Year's Eve party. I love this idea.

Being an avid biker, I want to invite everyone out to one of our local mountain bike skills parks, hire a food truck, and partner with a charity that provides bikes for kids in need. I'm planning to make it a yearly event in the spring or summer.

Let's Rev it Up!!!

Next Steps:

1. Revamp your review process and make a few requests from great past clients.
2. Review your past client referral strategy. Are you keeping in touch with them? What strategies can you implement soon?

Part 4: Ignition

Starting Up

Are you ready to fire up the engine and roar down the track yet?

As you can see by this point in the book, there's a lot to learn along this journey, and a lot of systems to build. If you're doing this all alone, from scratch, it's not going to be easy.

In fact, this may just be the hardest thing you've ever done. It certainly was for me. This path is only for the brave!

However, because I want the best for you, I feel compelled to also share a fallback option with you. Being the independent, hard charging, Single Agent is not the only way to start your career. In fact, my first successes came not as a solo agent, just me against the world. Rather, I first found real success within the shelter and structure of a team.

It was already a well oiled machine before I arrived. Leads showed up daily. There was a process and accountability for follow up. The sales process was documented and coached. My time was freed up to simply serve the needs of my clients without too much outside work. The company transaction coordinator handled everything from contract to close. And the company made sure the clients left reviews.

I understand how overwhelming it can be to build all of this from scratch, all by yourself. Joining an existing team that already has all of these pieces in place can be a huge advantage. You would be far more successful on a great team than trying to operate by yourself with half-built systems.

On a great team, the leads come to you and all you need to do is serve them. You're free from building all the business systems and it feels more like having a job than being an entrepreneur. Plus, you'll learn how each piece of the business operates, and if you ever decide to venture out as a single agent in the future, you'll be miles ahead of your competition.

I mention this option not because I don't believe in you. I know if you commit to the systems in this book, they will work for you. It works. I mention the team option because I see too many good agents who've tried to make a go of it alone, then get discouraged and leave the business.

I'd rather see you be successful on a team for a few years before transitioning to solo, than to see you fail out of the business like 87% of your peers. In fact, I think more agents should start out that way. These systems can be built on the side, over time, leading to your ultimate success as a single agent.

In the Conclusion of this book, I'll go more into detail about the team structure I created to help new agents, as well as why I think it's an important concept for the industry to move toward. I'll share the passion that lead me to build The LoneRock Home Team.

So, either join a high-producing team, or fully commit to building each Cylinder of your Real Estate Business with speed and tenacity. Don't lolligag in between. That's where real estate careers go to die. Don't half ass it. Do not allow yourself to drown from inaction. Commit to one of those two courses of action, and get to work! Hit it with everything you've got.

Now, with that caveat out of the way, if you're dead set on going full speed into single agent mastery, here's what I'd recommend:

162

Structure

The first thing to conceptualize is where your business sits in the landscape of other companies all serving the same real estate clients. Above you sits your brokerage. Then, in the middle is your Agent business, as an independent contractor to the brokerage. Below you, there are various Leveraged Services that you can hire to help service your clients. These can be automations (like CRMs and software), people (like assistants or transaction coordinators), or companies (like a photo/video company or marketing agency.) Then beside you are other companies your client hires like lenders, title, attorneys, inspectors, etc. I think of these as Partners or Preferred Vendors.

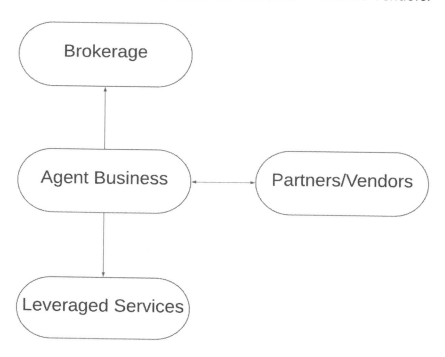

All of these connections make up part of the structure of your business. All should be chosen carefully. All should be held to high standards.

Brokerage

Let's start with the brokerage you decide to work with. First and foremost, their **Values** should align with your own. Do they put the client first, or is company profit their central concern? Do they encourage creative marketing and client programs, or do they require more top down control? How do you feel when you hear announcements from the founders or management? Are they warm and personable or cold and aloof?

Make sure it feels like the right fit for you.

Secondly, how about your **Peers**? Are there top producing agents you can learn from at the brokerage? Are they open to meeting with you and mentoring you along the way? Is the culture competitive or cooperative amongst your peers?

Thirdly, you need to make sure the brokerage's **Profit Model** also allows you to profit as well. In my opinion, too many brokerages are charging too much for too little benefit. If a brokerage wants 33% or 50% of my commission, I'm going to expect a lot from them. That's getting into the territory of team splits, and so they'd better be providing leads, follow up systems, support, training, accountability, and complete transaction coordination. If it's anything less than that, I personally wouldn't be able to justify that expense.

At this point, I need to brag on the brokerage I've had the pleasure of working with for most of my career, **Fathom Realty**. My experience here has been incredible. From the founder, Joshua Harley, all the way down to every support staff member

I've ever interacted with, the company exudes a heart of service. The brokerage is truly there to serve the needs of the agents and their clients.

I have several top producing agents I'm fortunate enough to call great friends, both locally and nationally within the Fathom brand. It's a great group of people to be associated with.

The technology is amazing as well, starting with the flagship intelliAgent software which handles all of our contract files and data. It also functions as a website builder, marketing platform, and CRM. It has more functionality than you'll ever need. Then we also have tremendous training opportunities within the brokerage's platform. There are also many assets like buyer and seller guides as well as marketing tools available to the agents as well.

In addition to all that, the fees are some of the lowest in the industry, which allows me to pour my profits back into marketing, consistently growing my agent business in a predictable manner. This fee structure has been instrumental in allowing me to scale. I wouldn't have been able to double-double-double without it.

If you'd like to check out Fathom Realty, just reach out to me at the contact form on www.LoneRockHomeTeam.com/AgentResources and I will personally introduce you to the District Director nearest you.

Your Business

Your business consists of all the systems contained within the 6 Cylinders we've discussed here in this book. This includes your ad campaigns, your follow up funnels, your sales skillset, your level of service, your contract-to-close process, and your past client relations. It also includes all the assets you build along the way, such as educational videos, PDFs, printed materials, and other types of information transfer.

Leverage (Automated Systems, Outsourced Services, Employees)

As you scale your business, it will also start to include many different types of leverage, allowing you to spend less time on each cylinder of the business and efficiently streamlining your efforts. Utilizing leverage frees you up to spend more time prospecting for business, developing content & campaigns, and actually serving clients.

"From a young age, I learned to focus on the things I was good at and delegate to others what I was not good at. That's how Virgin is run. Fantastic people throughout the Virgin Group run our businesses, allowing me to think creatively and strategically."

– Richard Branson

One of the best uses of leverage is **Automation**, such as automated email campaigns through a CRM. Other types of leverage include **Outsourcing** to service providers such as photographer/videographers to help create marketing content. A transaction coordinator is another great example of outsourced leverage. Still yet, as you expand, you may actually hire **Employees** and put them on a payroll to help free up more of your time. This could be the case for assistants, social media managers, or ISAs (Internal Sales Agents) to help with follow up and conversion.

Partners

There are many peripheral businesses to yours within the real estate industry, and hired by the same clients. These relationships are crucial for the fulfillment of good real estate services to your clients. You'll work hand in hand with other business and service providers hired by your clients such as lenders, attorneys, and title companies. These are all your Vendor Partners we discussed in **Cylinder #4: Service- Showing and Listing.**

Goals

Going back to the **3 A's Principle** (Acquisition-Alignment-Accuracy), creating a Goal for your business is vitally important to your success. Without a target to hit, you'll never know whether you're succeeding or not. You'll just be lost in the chaos of the moment with no clear direction.

Goals should be written like this:

> **-Present Tense,** not in the future. Not "I *will* achieve"... but simply "I achieve..." Present, not future tense. It's more active and immediate for your mind to grasp.

> **-Measurable –** You should know whether you've hit it or not without ambiguity. This should be reduced to a numerical metric. Numbers are quick and easy to measure.

-Timed – Without committing to a specific timeline, the goal is open ended and could always be procrastinated. A goal without a deadline is just a wish, a hope that it will happen someday. State which day it will be accomplished by.

A correctly stated goal should follow this formula:

"I accomplish X result by Y time."

My preference is to state goals in half the time that most people would want to accomplish them. **I prefer 6 month goals** instead of 12 month or yearly goals. It forces me into action more quickly and doesn't allow time to procrastinate. Even if you have a yearly goal, it may be helpful to break it up into a "by July" and a "by January" goal.

For instance, here's a great goal:

"I close 9 transactions by July of 20XX."

You may also find it helpful to consider a "Run Rate" goal, especially when scaling up your business (more on that in the next chapter). I try to get a consistent number of closings happening every month, and I often call this a "Run Rate." That goal structure might read like this:

"I achieve a Run Rate of 2 closings/mo. by July 20XX"

Then you'll Align your Action Steps to get there.

Plan, Budget, Schedule

From this main goal, I typically like to break down what actions are required to accomplish this goal. This is the **Alignment phase of the 3 A's.**

*-What **advertising campaigns** will I need to run?*
Make that a monthly goal.

"I create 1 Homes List ad and 4 video ads by January 31, 20XX"

*-**How many leads** will I need to bring in to accomplish this?*

Make that a monthly goal as well.

"I collect 100 leads by January 31, 20XX"

*-**How many follow up calls** should I make to properly help those leads?*
Perhaps that should be a weekly goal.

"I perform 50 Follow Up attempts by next Monday."

These goals should be reviewed at least every week, but preferably every morning before starting work. Then I schedule my day to include at least a few steps toward bigger goals along with all my other daily tasks.

I like to schedule quarterly projects to build assets and programs. I also schedule out monthly content campaigns, and place them into my calendar. Likewise, I build in time for my weekly follow up & reach outs.

Legal, Accounting, and Taxes

No part of this book should be construed as legal or tax advice.

You should have your own attorney and CPA to consult with all legal and tax questions.

Make sure to discuss the pros and cons of operating as an LLC versus a sole proprietor. What are the legal protections? What are the tax benefits?

I've chosen to operate as an LLC in order to separate my ad campaign budgets from my personal credit. When launching a new ad campaign, it's sometimes difficult to pay for it all outright, and using credit is helpful until I can pay it off with the transaction volume the campaigns generate. I feel confident with the investment of capital because I know my metrics and the expected return on ad spend. However, I don't like carrying high balances on personal credit cards even temporarily, as it drags my credit score down. But, corporate credit cards don't affect my personal score in the same way. Corporate cards can often keep higher balances without penalty. In fact, using the business cards, frequently spending and paying off the balances looks good for the business' credit.

In addition to those credit benefits, my business can purchase office equipment, marketing materials, and even vehicles, all with corresponding tax benefits. I can pay myself with a regular salary from my business as a W2 employee (taxed at a higher rate) and keep the rest of the profits in the business where it's susceptible to a lower "corporate income" tax rate.

As you can see, the benefits are worth exploring. For my business, it was worth starting an LLC to operate under, especially as I've moved to running a team, not just remaining as a solo agent. Again, please rely on your own tax and legal counsel for the best advice specific to your jurisdiction.

Let's Rev it Up!!!

Next Steps:

1. Review the business structure.
   a. Are you happy with your current brokerage?
   b. What types of leverage can you improve with?
   c. Do you have all the vendor connections you need?
2. Have you done you have a Goal Setting session? Get really clear about your goals and action steps.
3. Set a plan, budget, and schedule for completion.
4. Book appointments with your legal and tax professionals.

Part 5:
Shifting Gears

Scaling Up

When moving your business from one level to the next, it's helpful to view this like shifting gears. When ramping up to the next phase, you'll need to "Gas it!" right before you launch into that next level. This means you'll need to be saving some of the profits from the current phase and keeping them in reserves to launch the next round of advertising campaigns.

At each level, you'll need to establish the ideal **Run Rate** (Number of Closings per Month), so you know you've firmly established yourself in that higher gear. This is why Run Rate goals, not totals are often more helpful during your "scaling up" process. Then save as much of those profits as you can, so you can Double the Ad Spend in the next level up.

This is why I gravitate toward 6 month goals as well. It often takes 3-4 months to see the return from ad campaigns and follow up actions. So it might take until month 4, 5, and 6 to really see the Run Rate get established at the appropriate level. Then by month 7, it's often possible to double the ad spend again.

So, starting the scale up process at the beginning of a year might include a series of goals like this:

"I establish a Run Rate of 1 closing/mo. by July, 20XX."

Then, if you accomplish that Run Rate during April, May, and June, ramp it up for the next 6 months.

"I establish a Run Rate of 2 closings/mo. by Jan., 20XX."

If the end of that year goes as planned, shift gears into the New Year.

"I establish a Run Rate of 4 closings/mo. by July, 20XX."

With that cadence in mind, take a look at the following business structures, and notice the way campaigns, automations, and outsourcing can grow as your business (and budget) grows. This is very similar to what I did when growing my business from the ground up. However, I have removed services I paid for that didn't work, and systems I wouldn't use again if I had to do it all over.

This first example is a Run Rate of only 1 Closing for every 2 months, or 6 Closings/Year. Unfortunately, this is the average number of closings across our industry, so I think this should be the very first goal. Let's call this first gear.

First Gear - Level 1

3 Listings per Year
(~1 per Quarter)
3 Buyers per Year
$300,000 Avg.

$1,800,000 Volume
X 2.7% Commission
= $48,600 GCI

$6,000 Marketing

$6,000 BizEx/Systems

$36,600+ Net

Notice that this stage has a $500/month Marketing Budget ($6,000/yr). In order to scale from this stage, you should strive to save 3 months of the next highest marketing level. So, if you double it to $1,000/mo, we need to save an additional $3,000 for the first 3 months of our next level up. That's why I like to keep marketing expenses to about 25% of income. I strive to live on 50% (or Less) of my income. That allows me to scale up my ad campaigns with the other 25%.

It's a process of saving up marketing dollars for 3-6 months, then scaling up the campaigns for 3-6 months. Then once the deals from those campaigns start closing, the process starts all over. 6 months is about the fastest you should expect to move from level to level. It may take longer depending on market conditions and how aggressively you can save.

Second Gear - Level 2

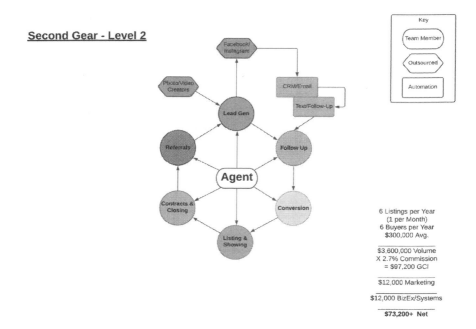

This second level is about double the average number of deals for agents in the US, and this is where it actually starts to feel like a decent income. Of course, you'll need to calculate the actual numbers for the average sale prices in your area and your typical commission. But in most areas, 12 deals per year should pay about as well as an average job in your locale.

Third Gear - Level 3

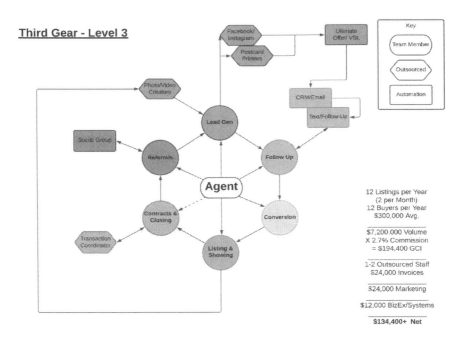

12 Listings per Year
(2 per Month)
12 Buyers per Year
$300,000 Avg.

$7,200,000 Volume
X 2.7% Commission
= $194,400 GCI

1-2 Outsourced Staff
$24,000 Invoices

$24,000 Marketing

$12,000 BizEx/Systems

$134,400+ Net

Level 3 is what many people actually aspire to when they start in real estate. It's that coveted "six figure" payout. At this level you should be able to start making some key outsourced hires like help with Marketing and Transaction Coordination. There is also sufficient room in the budget to start automating tasks by using Text/Follow-Up and Social Posting services. The more you automate and outsource during this time, the easier the next levels will come.

Fourth Gear - Level 4

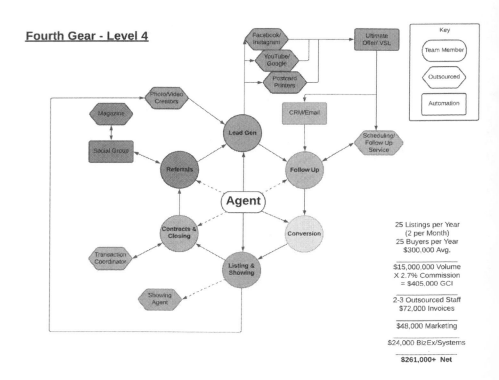

At this level, you could bring in a Showing Agent or Assistant, you can open up more Advertising channels, and hire more outsourced services. This level can make a quarter million dollars in my area. At this level, you're not just a real estate agent, you're a legitimate small business owner. You'll be making a very comfortable living which can transition into significant investments and eventually a very wealthy life.

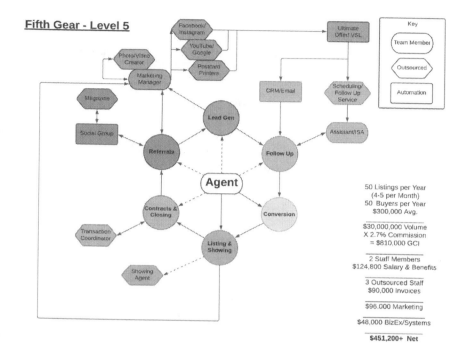

Fifth Gear - Level 5

This Fifth Gear, Level 5, can put an agent into the top 1% income bracket among all Americans, even in a lower priced market. In some markets, this 100 Deal/yr run rate would net over $1,000,000 per year.

As you can see, how fast and how far you **Scale Up** depends on how well you can shift your business into the next gear, and the next, and the next. I recommend you map out a trajectory similar to the plans in this chapter. I made all these charts with LucidChart.com. It's one of the most intuitive diagramming tools available. Play around with it and create your own structures and growth plans. This is how you **Supercharge your 6 Cylinder Business Engine** and start lapping the competition.

Part 6: Check the Gauges

Closings or Run Rate of Closings may be your goal, but due to the long transaction time in Real Estate, I find it helpful to use other metrics to monitor the ongoing health of my business. I think of these as the **Gauges of my Real Estate Race Car.** If closings are laps around the racetrack, the following metrics in this chapter let me know I'm on track for hitting my target lap time.

It's okay to keep the Closing goal at the forefront of your mind, but these metrics should be the main things you monitor on a weekly basis. They keep me accountable and honest with myself. If I'm not hitting these metrics, I won't hit the goal. There's no hiding from that truth. Either I'm putting in the work or I'm not. The closings won't happen without these preceding actions.

183

Speedometer = Advertising Impressions

The first metric you should be tracking is Advertising Impressions. This is the number of times your ads are being seen by your audience. This can include Facebook Homes List Impressions, Video Impressions, Post Card deliveries, Weekly Emails Sent, etc. I think of this as the **"Speed"** of my business.

20,000 Impressions per Week

It's important that this number maintain a consistent weekly and monthly cadence, with the number depending on the Level your business has attained. Ideally, this number will be at least as large as the number of people in your Alpha and Omega audiences. I like for them to see me on at least a bi-weekly basis, preferably every week. As those audiences grow, your expected weekly impressions should grow too.

Make sure to establish a goal **"Speed"** for your current business and create a chart to log the impressions across all advertising platforms. This chart will become the **"Speedometer" of your business.** Be sure to review it every week. Hold yourself accountable to delivering content to your audience.

You can find a sample "Agent Dashboard" at: www.LoneRockHomeTeam.com/AgentResources . You'll be able to edit and track your own numbers with the pre-made Google

Sheet we've prepared for you there. It includes Speedometer style gauges as well as a goal tracking chart like this:

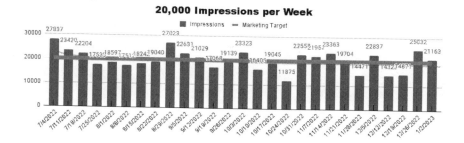

20,000 Impressions per Week

RPM = Reach Outs

    I often think of this next Gauge as the **"RPM."** On a car's dashboard, the RPM stands for Revolutions Per Minute, and that gauge tells you how hard the engine is working. I find it helpful to have an objective measure of how hard my business is working.

    The most impactful measure for this is how many times I'm reaching out to my leads in an attempt to help serve them. These one-to-one conversations are a lot of work, and the more of them I'm having on a weekly basis, the more real productivity I am accomplishing.

Complete 50 Reach Outs per Week

Actual Reach

0   100

52

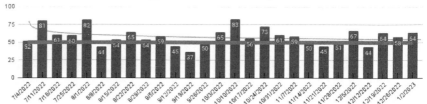

Complete 50 Reach Outs per Week

You can track this metric with number of phone dials, or number of conversations if you'd like. That's how we set up the Dashboard for you at www.LoneRockHomeTeam.com/AgentResources

But the number I actually use within our team is the Leaderboard number calculated in Follow Up Boss. We discussed this in **Cylinder #2: Follow Up.**

Within their algorithm, if you book an appointment, you automatically get 500 points. A phone conversation gives you 100 points. A phone call attempt (unanswered), gives 10 points. A text message is 2 points and an email is 1 point.

A week with 100 texts, 200 automated emails, 50 call attempts, 10 conversations and 2 booked appointments results in a **Score of 2900!** I find this is a very thorough metric and can be used effectively as my RPM Gauge. Plus, it's exciting to try and top last week's productivity number. Almost like winning a new high score on an arcade game. It's very engaging.

Interestingly, when you shift gears and jump up another level, your level of productivity may go up, even without as much effort on your part. For instance, when a new referral calls you at the recommendation of a cherished past client and you book an appointment with them, you just scored 500 points out of the blue. Your systems are literally doing that work for you. The same could happen when an Omega lead calls you from a Postcard.

Also, when you eventually outsource or hire someone to handle the follow up process, you'll still get to count their points for booked appointments, verification calls, and texts to those clients, even without much real work on your part. But it's still a true measure of how hard your business is working!

So again, figure out the baseline productivity you want to accomplish on a weekly basis, and then review your **Goal, "Speedometer", and "RPM"** gauges at the end of every week.

Conclusion

Which Route Will You Take?

Congratulations on making it this far! I appreciate the opportunity to share my journey with you and hopefully impart some knowledge along the way. We've explored important Mindset and Perspective Shifts. We've covered several direct methods of Lead Generation. We dove into the best practices for effective Follow-Up, and how to Convert those leads into clients. We discussed Showing and Listing property, along with writing a good Contract, and getting it to the Closing Table. Don't forget, we laid out simple methods to get great Reviews and Referrals.

You should also have a firm understanding of how to scale and grow your business from the ground up. You know the principle of reinvesting half of your profits, and doubling your results. At this point, you should have a clear growth path to the life and business you want.

Solo Vs. Team Leader

Not too long from now, when you've scaled up sufficiently, you'll have a major decision to make: do you continue as a Solo Agent (simply automating and outsourcing for efficiency), or do you build a Team of Agents and become a Team Leader. Both paths are respectable, and both can deliver tremendous results for your clients and for you.

As a Solo Agent, you'll keep more of your profits because you won't be splitting the commissions with other agents. You also get to make all the decisions yourself and don't have to worry about managing a team. On the downside, it can be tough to handle a lot of clients on your own and you might feel a little lonely without anyone to bounce ideas off of. Plus, taking time off or taking on new projects can be a challenge.

On the other hand, being a team leader has its benefits too. You have a team to help you out and handle a bigger workload, and you can focus on the big picture and delegate tasks to others. You also get to be a mentor and provide support to your team members. However, being a team leader also comes with extra responsibilities like managing and leading the team. Another downside is that you'll have to split your commissions with your team members. Plus, you might have less control over the day-to-day operations of the business and less direct client interaction.

Partnership

If you're at the very beginning and feeling overwhelmed, or you'd like some help getting your career started, remember the **Team Option**. As mentioned before, my career really took off when I joined a team and learned all aspects of the business from the inside out. I understand the leg up you can get with the help of a good mentor and a great team of other professionals to learn from.

I encourage you to view this option as a Partnership. You are literally partnering with a high-producing team leader who has already built the business systems you will need to thrive. However, their business won't work unless you're successful. They're truly invested in your success.

That's why, as soon as I had grown to a fairly high production level on my own, I decided that I would start a team.

I'm passionate about mentoring agents to success through this unique team model, expanding on the 6 Cylinder System we discussed throughout this book. It's called the LoneRock Home Team.

If you're an agent in my local area of Northwest Arkansas, I'd love to sit down and have a cup of coffee/tea with you to discuss your goals and dreams. I'm always looking to partner with open minded, hard working professionals who love to serve clients at the highest level. If that's you, let's chat. Just contact me from the form on www.LoneRockHomeTeam.com/AgentResources .

I want to give back to other agents, and help them build the career they've always dreamed of, regardless of if we ever do business together or not. If you're an ambitious agent committed to your own success, partnering with a passionate team leader can make all the difference in getting your career going. The rest of your life will never be the same.

There are several positives to joining a real estate team, especially if you're a newer agent. Here are a few:

- **Training and support:** Real estate teams offer training and support to their newer agents, which can be especially helpful for those who are just starting out in the industry.
- **Networking opportunities:** Joining a real estate team can also provide you with the opportunity to network with more experienced agents and learn from them. This can be a valuable resource as you start building your own client base.
- **Collaboration and teamwork:** Working on a team can provide a sense of collaboration and support that can be helpful when you're just starting out. You can rely on the

expertise and assistance of your teammates as you navigate this complex world of real estate.

- **Increased visibility:** Being part of a real estate team can also increase your visibility in the market, as you'll be associated with an established brand and have access to the team's marketing resources. This can help you attract more clients and grow your business more quickly.
- **Accountability and Leadership:** Do you always do the work you tell yourself you'll do? Do you start working when you say you will? Make all the calls you say you will? If not, a great team leader can help you draw the best out of yourself, just like a personal trainer would help get you into shape in the gym. You still need to do the work, but you've always got someone who's cheering for you, and someone whom you don't want to let down.
- **Leads:** One potential benefit of joining a real estate team as a newer agent is that you may have access to leads provided by the team. This can be especially helpful if you're just starting out and don't yet have a strong network of your own.

Help with Lead Generation is the number one reason agents join teams. However, it's worth noting that the distribution of leads among team members can vary depending on the team and the specific arrangement. Some teams may have a more structured system for distributing leads, while others may be more informal. It's a good idea to discuss the lead generation process with the team leader or other team members to get a sense of how it works.

On the LoneRock Team, we distribute leads to all team members on a weekly basis, as long they are performing the appropriate follow-up with their current leads the prior week. Accountability to high-level service (especially Follow-Up procedures) is very important on our team. The RPM Gauge is reviewed every week, and high scores are rewarded with more opportunity.

Write Your Roadmap

In conclusion, being a real estate agent can be a rewarding and fulfilling career path. It requires hard work, dedication, and a willingness to constantly learn and adapt. While there are many paths to success in the industry, it's important to remember that your journey will be unique to you. By setting clear goals, developing a strong work ethic, and continually seeking out new learning opportunities, you can create your own roadmap to success in real estate. With the right mindset and approach, you can achieve your dreams and build a successful career in this field.

Don't be afraid to seek guidance and support from more experienced agents or mentors. They can provide valuable insights and advice as you navigate the industry. That's probably why you picked up this book, and it's something I've continuously done throughout my own career.

The real estate industry is constantly evolving, so it's important to stay up-to-date on the latest trends and best practices. Keep taking continuing education courses, attending industry events, and reading industry publications to stay informed. By continuously improving your skills and knowledge, you'll be well-positioned for long-term success in real estate.

Personal Invitation

Again, If you're an agent in NWA, I'd love to explore working together! I love connecting with like-minded, hardworking professionals. If that sounds like you, let's connect!

Just shoot me a message through the form on www.LoneRockHomeTeam.com/AgentResources, and we can set up a time to grab coffee and chat.

And if you're interested in more information about possibly joining our brokerage, Fathom Realty, no matter where you live in the USA, I'd be happy to connect you with the District Director nearest you. Simply contact me through the page above.

Or simply scan this QR code with your phone's camera:

Best wishes. Now crank that engine. **Let's REV IT UP!**

-Colley

Recommended Reading

The following books have made a huge difference in my life and business. I highly recommend you check them out:

The Compound Effect – Darren Hardy

The Talent Code – Daniel Coyle

The Slight Edge – Jeff Olson

Failing Forward – John C. Maxwell

How Life Imitates Chess – Garry Kasparov

The 4 Disciplines of Execution – McChesney, Covey, Huling

Sell 100+ Homes a Year – Krista Mashore

Defeat Mega Agents – Ryan Fletcher

$100M Offers – Alex Hormozi

80/20 Sales and Marketing – Perry Marshall

Influence: the Psychology of Persuasion – Robert Cialdini

Fanatical Prospecting – Jeb Blount

The 4:2 Formula – Jeff Shore

The Perfect Close – James Muir

Start With No – Jim Camp

Never Split the Difference – Chris Voss

Made in the USA
Columbia, SC
15 February 2023